"I was mesmerized by this book—I could not put it down. The concepts relating the brain to the development of the Internet were a combination of vision and science fiction. The anecdotes and examples are so compelling that you cannot stop reading until the last page."

—Pamela Goldberg, Program Director, Entrepreneurial Leadership
Program, Tufts University

"Wired for Thought is an important work for those executives who want both a framework for thinking about the Internet's potential and the context to understand why the great successes and failures of the web so far are just the beginning. Jeff Stibel takes you 'back to the future' with the first real look at how artificial intelligence will drive the way the Internet looks, feels, and functions . . . Web 3.0–6.0, here we come!"

—John Richards, former President, Starbucks N.A., Dean & DeLuca,
and Elizabeth Arden

"Finally, a science book that is readable, a business book that is interesting, and a technology book that is practical—all rolled into one. Stibel's important theories will help you understand how to harness the power of the ever-changing Internet for your business."

—Jeff Coats, retired Managing Director, GE Capital

"Jeff Stibel is the thinking man's Malcolm Gladwell. Understanding the concepts in *Wired for Thought* will go a long way to shaping the Obama administration's plan for digitizing medical information . . . just one application of this book's powerful thesis."

—Ron Ahrens, Board of Directors, CardioNet;
retired Chairman, Closure Medical

"Wired for Thought is a magical mystery tour for business readers covering cognitive science, evolution, linguistics, and neural science. Jeff Stibel predicts how the Internet is inevitably turning more and more into a global brain, and reading his book will give you insight into the principles of Web 4.0 to come."

—Jordan Pollack, professor of computer science, Volen Center for Complex
Systems, Brandeis University

"*Wired for Thought* is a major leap forward in evaluating the power of the Internet. By linking the Internet to the brain's complex functions and unique decision-making skills, Jeff provides us with insights that will change the way high-level executives prepare their organization for sustained success. This book is required reading for anyone in charge of business strategies who must think creatively about the future."

—Robert C. Blattberg, Timothy W. McGuire Distinguished Service Professor
of Marketing, Tepper School of Business, Carnegie Mellon University, and
author of *The Marketing Information Revolution* and *Customer Equity*

"*Wired for Thought* offers a rare opportunity to really understand the Internet and how to harness it. Stibel provides unique insights by lucidly combining cognitive neuroscience and the world of business."

—Itiel Dror, Principal Consultant, Cognitive Consultants International Ltd.
and psychology professor, University of Southampton

"In the 1930s, the French Jesuit and paleontologist Teilhard de Chardin wrote that humans would one day be connected by one central nervous system. Now Jeff Stibel has given that system a name—the Internet. By putting the familiar world of search engines and click-throughs into its proper historical and biological context, Stibel's book opens a whole range of fascinating possibilities and predictions about the future. Truly a work of philosophy and science, Stibel's *Wired for Thought* is also a practical business book, explaining how our collective brain will work in the future and how organizations can take advantage of it."

—Dick Morris, Chief Strategist to President Bill Clinton, and bestselling
author of *Behind the Oval Office*, *Outrage,* and *Fleeced*

"*Wired for Thought* is fascinating, fun to read, and very accessible. It gave me new insights and strengthened my understanding of both the brain and the Internet."

—Ellen Marram, Board of Directors, the *New York Times*,
Eli Lilly, and Ford; former President and CEO, Nabisco

Wired for Thought

Wired for Thought

How the Brain Is Shaping
the Future of the Internet

Jeffrey M. Stibel

With the collaboration of

Erik Calonius and Peter Delgrosso

HARVARD BUSINESS PRESS

Boston, Massachusetts

ISBN: 978-1-4221-4664-4

Library of Congress cataloging information available

The paper used in this publication meets the requirements of the American
National Standard for Permanence of Paper for Publications and Documents
in Libraries and Archives Z39.48-1992.

To Dennett and Lincoln

CONTENTS

BrainGate

I T IS IRONIC THAT MANY of humanity's achievements are rooted in a history of mistakes. This was true of Einstein's theory of relativity, many of the inventions of Thomas Edison, and numerous pharmaceutical drugs (such as penicillin and Viagra), and so, too, was it true of the most successful public offering in recent history.[1] Only weeks before Google's initial public offering in 2004, the company's founders made a critical error in judgment: they agreed to sit down for a magazine interview, something that typically is prohibited by the Securities and Exchange Commission (for fear that the information could be leaked or used to hype the stock). Beyond that, the interview was with *Playboy*, and that in and of itself was a bit troubling.[2]

But when SEC officials read the article, they dismissed it as harmless banter, clearing the way for one of the most successful IPOs in history.

Why did the SEC consider the article harmless? It was probably because one of Google's founders stated in the article that people would someday have direct access to the Internet through implants in their brains—allowing us to have "the entirety of the world's information as just one of our thoughts." That alone was likely enough for the SEC to assume that the founders of Google were nuts.

But the founders of Google aren't crazy. They understand both the Internet and the brain, and they know that an Internet implant could happen. The statement was forward thinking, certainly, but by no means foolish thinking. And as you read this book, you will quickly see that I share their enthusiasm for the convergence of the Internet and the brain. I even take their enthusiasm a few steps farther.

Imagine this: you are waking up. As your eyes focus, you see a white-haired man in a lab coat congratulating you on a successful surgery. You are still groggy from the anesthesia and can't quite remember what happened. The man enthusiastically explains that he is a scientist and that your surgery has previously been performed only on rats and rhesus monkeys. But with the help of a neurosurgeon, it has now been performed on yet another animal— a guinea pig—and that happens to be you.

Before you can gather your thoughts, the scientist makes an odd request: "Could you please turn off the lights?" As you look around the room, you don't see a light switch. But just as the thought crosses your mind, the lights go off. Smiling, he asks you to turn the lights back on. You think of it momentarily, and they snap on. He smiles again. "The brain implant has worked!"

If this scenario seems like science fiction, I assure you that it has far more science than fiction. In fact, this technology exists today. The scientist is John Donoghue, chair of the Neuroscience Department at Brown University. He, along with his colleagues, has invented an implantable device called BrainGate that allows people to use their minds to control electronics such as computers.

I was introduced to BrainGate when I began my doctoral program in cognitive science at Brown. As I soon learned, the brain uses electrical and chemical charges to communicate with itself and the rest of the body. The idea behind BrainGate is actually quite simple: by tapping in to the electrical charges of the brain, doctors can position them outward to control other electrical devices, in the same way your TV remote allows you to change the channel without leaving your couch. After numerous animal trials (if you imagine monkeys running down the hallowed halls of Brown turning out the lights using brain waves, you will not be far off), BrainGate was approved by the FDA for clinical trials on humans. The immediate goal was to provide more mobility for those with severe dysfunction, such as quadriplegics and Parkinson's patients.

Once I became familiar with these ideas, I urged one of Donoghue's students to start a company. That company was quickly funded by a venture capitalist.[3] It started human trials and quietly made its debut on the NASDAQ exchange a few years later.[4] The first clinical trial in 2004 involved a paralyzed man who is now able to control a computer cursor with his mind. The lead surgeon, another professor at Brown, described the results as "almost unbelievable."[5] I suspect he added the word "almost" out of deference to Donoghue. Four other patients have since been implanted, all with remarkable success. The results were published in the venerable journal *Nature* in 2006 (*Nature* had published the animal trials in 2002).[6]

Why does this story sound outrageous?[7] It is mainly because— as the doctor who performed the surgery has said—the idea is too hard to believe. We think of the brain as something beyond our comprehension, so we dismiss the notion that it obeys the laws of science. Here is the way CBS's *60 Minutes* put it when it featured BrainGate in 2008: "Once in a while, we run across a science story that is hard to believe until you see it. That's how we felt about this story when we first saw human beings operating computers, writing e-mails, and driving wheelchairs with nothing but their thoughts."[8]

The brain, however, is understandable. It is nothing more than a biological machine.

And that brings us back to the idea that the Google founders had. If we can implant a chip into our brains to turn on lights, can't we also implant a chip that allows us to remotely connect our brains to the Internet? That would give us access to virtually all of the world's information.

How would such a device affect what you think about memory? Would you still value rote memorization or be impressed by people who had photographic memories? Wouldn't you essentially have a perfect memory, limited only by your ability to retrieve information?

If you were able to connect to the Internet, you would also have access to millions of people, possibly through "mental" e-mail, Facebook, or instant messaging. If you couldn't find the information, you could ask someone, as if you were using a lifeline on *Who Wants to Be a Millionaire*. Would that change your notion of what intelligence is? Why value IQ when relationships are more powerful? After all, who is smarter when you have mental access to information—the person who knows all there is to know about quantum mechanics but nothing about nonlinear geometry, or the person who has close friends in both fields and just enough knowledge to ask the right questions? How would this kind of intelligence affect your personal life, your professional life, your business?

All this raises another, more important question: could the Internet itself be made to perform more like the brain? Could it perform the functions of a brain—just as a mechanical hearing aid performs the function of the inner ear, or a contact lens performs the function of the cornea, or an artificial heart performs the function of that biological muscle?

My conviction that the Internet is evolving into a brain has been the foundation of my business career. It has given me a way to anticipate what will happen next; it has given me vision. In many ways, because I understand the brain, I feel as if I'm seeing a movie for the second time when it comes to the Internet.

Why is this perspective important? It's because you could spend your entire life trying to understand each of the thousands of Internet companies that have sprouted. You could analyze the permutations of each of them. But if instead you understand the brain—how thinking works—you will understand what is happening on the Internet: not only what is happening now but also what will happen in the future.

You may ask what you will gain by reading this book. My answer is this: you can take any phenomenon and study its parts for years, but until you step back far enough to see it in its entirety you will not understand how it works and where it may go. If you do not understand energy on a global scale, you will not understand the business by studying wires and power plants. If you do not understand international agribusiness, you won't get anywhere standing in a field of corn. And this same principle is true of the Internet and the constellation of innovations and business opportunities that surrounds it.

The Internet Is a Brain

I N THE HISTORY OF LIVING THINGS, our species is unique in having invented devices that leverage and extend the powers of our own bodies. We have forged swords to extend the length and power of our arms; telescopes and cameras to extend the power of our eyes; artificial hearts to mimic the organic pumps that beat in our chests. We have come to understand that the human body can be reverse engineered. As Harvard psychologist Steven Pinker has said, "We understand the body as a wonderfully complex machine . . . The stuff of life turns out to be not a quivering, glowing, wondrous gel but a contraption of tiny jigs, springs, hinges, rods, sheets, magnets, zippers and trapdoors, assembled by a data tape (DNA) whose information is copied, downloaded and scanned."[1]

That description may be true of the body in general, but for a long time the brain was thought to be too mysterious to explain. We might create a pump in the image of the human heart, or a camera lens in the image of an eye, or even a hinge in the image of a bone joint. But what analogy could there be to the brain—a sticky, three-pound lump of wrinkled matter lying silently in the skull?

With computers, we have tried to find that analogy. We say that semiconductors switch on and off like neurons and that fibers of glass can transmit messages as do synapses and axons. Beyond that, however, we've come to a dead end. The computers we have built are not really as analogous to the human brain as, say, an artificial heart is to a real heart. A computer itself is not like a brain.

But then there is the Internet. With the Internet we have created something unlike anything humankind has built before. Steam locomotives, television sets, automobiles—they are all inert. Even chessboards and baseball stadiums, which flicker to life momentarily, go dark when the game is finished. But the Internet is not like that. It is unbounded, self-perpetuating, and capable of collective consciousness. It is more like the crowd in the baseball stadium than the ball game, more like the gambits of chess than the chessboard and the rules.

To be sure, every significant innovation is miraculous—a discovery that is more than the sum of its parts. Alexander Graham Bell attached two small drums to two solenoids, for instance, and out of those bits created something beyond the sum of the parts: transmission of the human voice. But the telephone did not go on to replicate and improve itself, by itself; the Internet can and does. And beyond that, the Internet learns. It processes information, shapes it, transmits it. It remembers some things, forgets others, and constantly loops whatever it has, spinning it in as many ways and as many directions as one could imagine.

For these reasons (and many more, as you will read in this book), I offer you this simple analogy: as the artificial pump is to the heart, as the camera is to the eye, and as the hinge is to the joint, I believe that the Internet is to the brain. In fact, I'll go one better than that. I believe that the Internet *is* a brain.

At first blush, that assertion may seem preposterous. The Internet is a brain? When I say the Internet is a brain, I don't mean that the Internet is that three-pound glob, all wrinkled like your toes when you climb out of a hot bath. I mean that the Internet is gradually gaining the ability to think. Now before you decide I'm writing the screenplay for a B-grade science fiction thriller, let me do some explaining. To understand why I believe that the Internet is a brain, you must first understand how I define the brain itself.

A Paper Model of the Brain

Most of my friends get their weekly dose of medical science from *Grey's Anatomy* and *ER*, so it is no surprise that they think of the brain as a sticky hunk of gray matter that looks like a chewed-up football. In reality the brain is nearly 60 percent white matter, with only the remainder being the gray stuff we typically think of. Except for the brain's deep ridges and two hemispheres, most people wouldn't recognize a brain if they were sitting next to one in an airport terminal. The brain is actually very soft, almost jellylike, ivory in color with deep red veins—more Bordeaux than Burgundy. The firm, gray brains we think of don't take on that form until they are actually dead, bloodless, preserved, and of little use to us (see figure I-1).

But even that description is misleading. In the way it thinks, the brain is far more similar to a legal-sized piece of paper (so I guess my friends would have been better off getting their science

FIGURE I-1

Picture of exposed meninges and brain during surgery (awake craniotomy)

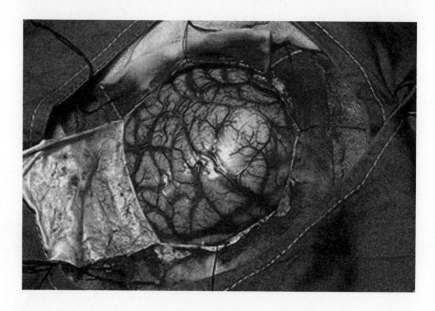

Source: Reproduced with permission from Dr. Emil A. Popovic, MD (www.popovic.com.au).

from *L.A. Law* or *Law & Order)*. This piece of paper represents the outermost area of the brain, the *cerebral cortex*. It is here that most of the magic of thought takes place. Imagine this piece of paper: thin, rectangular, and blank (mostly) to start.[2] On the paper are bits of information that grow, like Braille embossed on the page, as the brain is formed. Those are the *neurons*, the brain's computing units, and they help to store and process information.

But what's intriguing is how the brain was designed physically to connect information. Suppose you place a number of dots at random on the page; if you imagine two dots at either end, they are far away from each other. Now if you crumple the paper into a ball, the two dots grow closer. If you crumple the page enough times, each point will be within striking distance of every other point. Now you really understand the brain: it is uniquely powerful, because it enables connections between disparate pieces of information. It allows for quick communication. The brain is not fast in general—at least not compared with computers—but it makes up for its lack of speed by packing information tightly inside our skulls, like the crumpled paper.

From a computing standpoint, the human brain is a sophisticated *parallel processing* machine. This means that unlike *serial* computing—in which one thing happens, then another, and then another—in parallel processing a number of things can be happening at once. Neuroscientists call this *distributed computing*, meaning that because the functions of the brain are distributed all over the place, things happen simultaneously. (I think that *distributed computing* is a better term, because *parallel computing* conjures the idea of two unbending parallel lines—like railroad tracks—whereas *distributed* is a freewheeling image that describes more accurately how the brain actually works.)

A Brief History of the Brain

Six million years ago our brains were the size of chimps' brains. No surprise, these primitive brains gave us a chimp-like level of intelligence. But about 2.5 million years ago we had what has been dubbed "the Great Encephalization."[3] Over the next 150,000 years, our brains grew by 400 percent. This was good: as a result, not only were we hardwired to avoid danger (instinctively jumping out of the way), but also we had acquired a sense of anticipation (so that we could suspect that a four-legged creature with fangs was up to no good).

But something even better was beginning to happen: the human brain began to develop its *cerebral cortex*, a one-eighth-inch mantle of about 10 billion neurons that, like a shower cap, fit tightly over the primitive brain. The cerebral cortex added another dimension to human intelligence: reasoning, introspection, and even the refined elements of emotion.

Now the human brain has about 100 billion neurons, or, as one researcher noted, the equivalent surface area of roughly four football fields (in comparison, the base of the great Pyramids in Egypt would only cover ten football fields).[4] Neurons consist of the soma, an axon, and dendrites. Think of the *soma* (and its nucleus) as the center of the neuron, or the information clearinghouse. The *axon* acts as a transmitter, sending information from one neuron to another. The *dendrites* receive information from other neurons. Neurons communicate with one another through electrical and chemical transmitters. Tightly packed, neurons work together in a distributed network, forming patterns that allow us to perform tasks such as walking, speaking, remembering someone's name, and even reading this book.

The most amazing fact about the brain, however, is that the brain is not very amazing. Like the rest of our bodies, it's made up of humble carbon molecules. There's no magical goo anywhere—no special place where our thoughts reside, not to mention our desires, ambitions, fears, dreams, aspirations. The brain is only a lump of axons and dendrites and other carbon-based stuff. For all my years in graduate school and all the books I've read on the brain, there ain't much more to it than that.

A Sacred Chalice

The fact that the brain is an ordinary organ—it's got nothing over the pancreas or the liver downtown—is actually a good thing in terms of trying to create an artificial mind. The brain's very ordinariness frees us to speculate that an intelligent Internet is possible. Does that sound somewhat sacrilegious? To be sure, the brain is a sacred organ in a sacred chalice, but to many philosophers, scientists, and more than a few Internet moguls, the idea of mechanized thinking is no longer beyond the question, "Why not?"

This brings us to the Internet, which, as it turns out, is very similar in structure to the brain. The Internet is a massive storage and retrieval system. In practice, it is clunkier and smaller than the brain (neurons versus computers, not sheer size or weight), but the fundamental structure is roughly the same. As shown in figure I-2, the brain has neurons and memories; the Internet has computers and Web sites (these are connected together through Ethernet cables and hyperlinks instead of axons and dendrites).

FIGURE I-2

The neurons of the brain (left) and the computers of the Internet

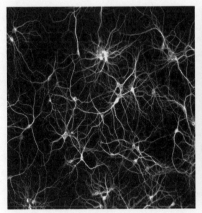

Source: Image (at left) courtesy of Paul De Koninck, www.greenspine.ca; image (at right) courtesy of the Opte Project through the Creative Commons license, http://creativecommons.org/licenses/by-nc-sa/1.0/.

It's true that something may look like something else and not be analogous. The switching yard at a railway station looks something like a brain network, but it isn't. Yet there are things about the Internet that make its similarity to the brain too strong to resist.

The Internet is really the combination of two innovations. The first was the telegraph (the precursor to the telephone), which allowed information to be transmitted electronically. With the advent of the telegraph, people could communicate instantaneously across enormous distances and through the most difficult terrain. This capability seems obvious to us now, but it was unimaginable during the days of the Pony Express.

The second innovation was the computer, which allowed information to be processed and stored. Before the computer, information was processed using calculating devices and then written down on paper. Before the computer, complex calculations—the type even the most modest laptop does without breaking a sweat— were virtually impossible. And if valuable or large amounts of information—say, a book manuscript—needed to be stored, the best place to put it was under a mattress or in a bank.

Both the telegraph and the computer solved huge problems, but combining the two created new opportunities. The Internet was the result. The modern-day Internet is simply a network of computers hooked together by telegraph lines (or what we think of now as phone, broadband, or cable lines). It started with two connected locations and has grown to hundreds of millions.[5] This simple, yet powerful amalgamation allows us to store, process, and transmit information.

When you plug your computer in to the wall, it is connected to all the computers at Yahoo! and Facebook and MIT, and your computer is as much a part of the Internet as are these institutions. What makes the Internet powerful are the hundreds of millions of computers connected to each other, all sharing information, computing and working on your behalf as you sit in your house searching for "vegan brownie recipes" on Google. As with the brain, this means that the Internet, too, can process information in parallel. A lot has been said about the Internet, but nothing more is needed to understand it.

Taking Flight

That's why I say that the Internet today is a replica of the brain: computers and microchips represent neurons (the soma or calculating unit); like memory in the brain, Web sites house information; links among pages build semantic maps; and like axons and dendrites, phone lines carry that information across multiple regions. We are in the early stages, of course, but look at the growth: in its first ten years, the World Wide Web grew at roughly 850 percent per year.[6]

The human brain has more than 100 billion neurons. In another twenty years or so, the number of computers connected to the Internet will equal that number. In time, I believe the Internet will approximate the complexity of the brain. Think of it this way: evolution took hundreds of thousands of years to evolve the human brain to its current level of complexity and sophistication. The Internet will approximate that in a few generations. We will have experienced in cyberspace a replication of biological growth itself, as though it were the brain of a living thing. But more to the point, we will replicate not only the brain itself but also its by-product: thought.

This development is not unlike the evolution of flight. When the Wright brothers first flew (an attempt that most people had considered lunacy until the Wright Flyer actually lifted off, and even then most thought it was a stunt), their intent was not to create a bird. To be sure, some innovators thought that building a "bird" was the road to flight, but it was not. The Wright brothers harnessed the laws of flight, and not the body of a duck or a blue jay. The reporters who covered those early attempts didn't report breathlessly, "Yep, every year these things are getting to look more and more like ducks. Seems like they'll have the beak pretty well worked out in a few months and the tail feathers perfected next year." The truth is, flying might have been in the realm of the birds, but humanity was going to accomplish flight in its own way. And we did achieve flight on our own terms, without replicating what nature had done.

The same can be said of Internet intelligence. It will no more look like a brain than an airplane looks like a bird. Nor it is going to act like a human being.

And let me add an important (albeit subtle) thought about the term *artificial intelligence*. This term has been around since the 1950s, and it tends to conjure images of robots. But let me assure you that when we create a "thinking machine," there will be nothing "artificial" about the intelligence. Yes, the machine may be artificial, but the intelligence will be real. The term has done more harm than good and should be banished, so you will not find the term *artificial intelligence* in this book. Think of it this way: my grandmother has an artificial hip; the hip is artificial, but the ability to walk is real. The same will be true of the intelligence behind the Internet.

If you remember that the first Wright Flyer flew a shorter distance than the length of today's 747s, you can appreciate the idea that when we do get the Internet to think (and I believe we already have) it will be in a very small way—at first. And from there, you will see businesses blossom and billions of dollars' worth of value created, just as it happened in the airline industry.

The Business of the Brain

I don't know where the Internet will be in fifty years. But I do see where it will be in the next ten to twenty years, and I'm certain that it will be built on the concepts of brain science. Many of the other players in this industry foresee the same thing. It's no coincidence that Google's Larry Page and Sergey Brin not only studied artificial intelligence at Stanford under Terry Winograd, a brilliant leader in that field, but also put those lessons to work in shaping and developing their company. (In fact, Google's eighteenth employee was a brain surgeon, and he became Google's operations chief.)[7]

It's also no coincidence that brain science is the secret strategy behind most other Internet businesses—companies like Amazon.com, Yahoo!, Google, Microsoft, and Facebook. This is why many of these companies have the same brain scientists on their staffs as are found at Stanford, Brown, MIT, and Harvard. The fact is that most successful Internet companies are premised, either explicitly or implicitly, on the conviction that the Internet is evolving to become more and more like a brain.

The evolution of this phenomenon has been fast. Ten years ago no one would have imagined that software programs could be developed remotely by thousands of independent programmers.

But in hindsight it is obvious after seeing the success of Linux, the open-source software that has been developed not by a company but by millions of users. Five years ago no one would have imagined that an encyclopedia could be developed by millions of participants and still hold fast to its independence. But that is happening now with Wikipedia. Nor should it be a surprise to learn that games, furniture, communities, and Pulitzer Prize-winning novels will be developed that way in the next ten years.

No one would have believed that simulated communities would thrive in cyberspace to the extent that they are. But if the Internet is evolving as a brain with millions of people interacting and developing that brain, then it is the perfect environment for such things to flourish. These are intelligent actions by a fledgling Internet. Those in the business world who are waiting for the Internet to behave like a human being—or feel that thinking can't be created without a robot of some kind arriving deskside with a martini—will miss out on these opportunities, and many more.

With this insight, in fact, my teams have helped develop Internet companies worth hundreds of millions of dollars. It's this insight that led my colleagues and me to create an Internet version of a technology called WordNet, which now underlies Google's advertising system (AdSense). And it is this insight that led me to BrainGate, the technology that is now connecting humans to computers by implanting computer chips into people's brains.

Moreover, it's an insight that will help my team and others in the future to build businesses worth far more than these. Why? It's because once you recognize that the Internet is a brain, you can to some extent see where it is going. Numerous aviation companies were started after the Wright brothers' first flight, and most of them failed. But the technology of flight moved on. We have the same phenomena now—the same growth and growing pains of a new industry—but this time with thinking machines rather than flying machines.

That's why I know where it is going next—and why I have some expectation as to where I will be in the next few years, as I build one new company after another. The inevitability is no less obvious to me than that of American railroads pushing west in the nineteenth century. And by absorbing these ideas, you will position yourself a few miles down the track—set up a depot and a water tower—and have it ready when they get there.

A Few Big Ideas

I have made some bold statements; you are skeptical. It is my task to convince you that my conjectures are true (and perhaps even conservative). Between the covers of this book are some unusual ideas. They aren't conventional thoughts. But if you are ready for a fresh perspective on the Internet—for ideas that will help you think about the Internet in a new way—then here they are:

- The Internet is a brain. By this I mean that the Internet is more than a reflection of intelligence; it actually manifests intelligence. This is because the Internet (unlike computers) has evolved with many of the same basic structures and abilities as a brain. You may argue that "is a brain" and "is like a brain" are merely a matter of semantics, but subscribing to either version will help you better understand the Internet.

- The human brain is rather dumb—but that is precisely why it's so smart. The Internet, unlike mighty supercomputers, was built with many of the same weaknesses that enable human intelligence. Humanlike thinking will not come from creating more powerful computers or building on the strength of artificial intelligence, but rather from a network approach that mimics the *weaknesses* of human thinking.

- The history of technology is not really a history but an evolution—one machine supplanting another in a Darwinian race for dominance. The history of the Internet takes things one step further: here we have an evolution that is in fact an extension of the evolution of the human brain.

- Although the brain is a poor calculating machine, it is a pretty efficient prediction machine. Although a human brain cannot calculate a mathematical equation as quickly as even the most basic calculator, it can easily determine where a ball in midflight will land without calculating its precise trajectory or velocity. The brain functions very differently from computers, but it functions in a manner similar to the way the Internet works.

- Just as human intelligence is a matter of creating and destroying memories and ideas, so is the Internet a machine that creates only to destroy. And the creative destruction underlying memories is the driving force behind the World Wide Web.

- Language is an attribute that many consider uniquely human, but it is at the heart of the most popular and important tool on the Internet: search.

- Inevitably, the Internet will crash. But it will get better and stronger with each collapse. In fact, all networks stop growing in size, but in so doing they grow in wisdom and strength. Similarly, by childhood, you will have lost most of the neurons that grew during your infancy. And as an adult, your brain continues to shrink. But as the number of neurons in your brain decreases, your wisdom increases.

- The Internet may never be "conscious" in the human sense (and who needs it?), but it will be (and already is) capable of creating a collective consciousness. This, to a great extent, accounts for the success of the Internet.

Never before has the idea of a thinking machine brought together a greater confluence of thinkers and scientists. This includes neurologists, who are dissecting the brain with greater skill and advanced instruments; psychologists, who are coming to understand behavior that emerges from the brain; linguists, who recognize how thoughts are put into the symbols that we call words; evolutionary scientists, who are cracking into a new field of computer science called genetic algorithms; computer scientists, who (with the understanding given them by psychologists and others) are building machines and algorithms that mimic the mind; and artificial intelligence types, who are focusing intently on getting machines to actually think.[8]

There are also a number of brain scientists who are experts in both the brain and in the philosophy of thought—people like my mentors Dan Dennett (my daughter's name is Dennett, as an homage to him) and Jim Anderson (I don't have an Anderson . . . yet). Dennett, considered one of the greatest living philosophers, has chronicled and plumbed the questions of the mind in a series of groundbreaking books. Anderson, a leading brain scientist at Brown, is working to build the underlying mechanism. In writing this book, I stood on these broad shoulders—and I do not shy away from saying that the deepest thoughts and the clearest conjectures are theirs, not mine.

Of course, even among this group of distinguished thinkers, there is no consensus. The field of thought from which this book emerges is more circus than cerebral. Dan Dennett, in *Consciousness Explained* (a book the *New York Times* cited as one of the ten best of the year when it was published in 1991) notes, "No one can keep all the problems clear, including me, and everyone has to mumble, guess, and hand wave about large parts of the problem."[9] Should I fail to be perfectly clear in the pages that lie ahead—not that I won't try to be clear—let that serve as my apology as well.

The voices may be many and the opinions sharply different, but in this newly opening world of brain science and technology, we are finally seeing a convergence on the idea that a thinking machine is as inevitable as was the first flying machine.—And consequently, that this newfound intelligence will affect all parts of our lives. For that reason, I have written this book for a broad audience.

In particular, though, I have written it with the business world in mind. For this is the sector of society, as it was when the Wright brothers first flew, that will build these pioneering ideas into an industry. Most businesspeople have never heard of such pioneers as Alan Turing or John von Neumann, let alone Jim Anderson or Dan Dennett. Most don't understand what distributed computing is or the significance of the way Internet companies rise and fall.

I constantly hear people speaking about the Internet in terms of servers, PCs, software, HTML, and Ethernet. I hear others talking about the business components—who's on first at Google, Yahoo!, and the like. But only a handful of people have stepped back far enough to ask, What does this really mean? These few are largely those who have studied, or at least understand, brain science. We see the Internet as more than the newest thing in telecommunications, just as some people saw airplanes as more than the newest thing in steam locomotives. The Internet is transformational. It is the first real replication of the human brain, outside the human body, that we have seen.

How does this insight give you competitive advantage? Within these pages, we will certainly examine the specifics, such as how it helps you make better Web sites and optimize your online advertising. But the more important advantage is that it gives you vision. It gives you the ability to stand slightly ahead of the current business ferment, build a new business model, and wait for other businesses to catch up.

But first, the quest for humanlike intelligence requires an initial step: an exploration into how we, as human beings, think. It takes a bit of homework, to be sure, but the background reading in the next few chapters will be invaluable as you apply that knowledge to the practical elements of the Internet later in the book. We can't create intelligence, after all, until we understand what thinking is all about.

So what goes on when we think? When we make decisions? When we respond to the world around us? To answer these questions, accompany me to a cow pasture, where we may find some answers.

PART I

Building
the Brain

CHAPTER 1

The Thinking Machine

CLOSE YOUR EYES and imagine a purple cow. Now close your eyes and imagine a yellow cow. Where did these thoughts come from? How did they get there? Is there a place in your brain that stores cow images, and another with an inventory of paint cans with which to color them? These are important questions, because before we can create something that thinks, we must understand how we think.

Supercomputers can search billions of records in a fraction of a second. They can remember hundreds of billions of facts perfectly. They can even power up their electric circuits to react at least a million times as fast as the neurons in our brains.

Pretty smart, huh? So all we have to do is build more of those industrial-size microprocessor farms, packed with supercomputers, and someday we'll have human intelligence capable of imagining purple cows. Right?

No. Not really. In fact, not at all.

The truth is that a supercomputer is too good to behave like a human brain. A computer could never answer or even imagine the purple cow question. It is too precise, too correct, too predictable, too Miss Goody Two-Shoes. The computer is like the ticking of a Swiss watch, and the human brain is more like a blues note on a bender.

To behave like the human brain, a computer would have to behave like this: start searching for an item with fierce concentration, then back off a little, then jump back in, then find itself staring blankly out the window (assuming there is a window), then off to a warm reverie—shafts of sunlight bouncing off the green grass or something like that—and then suddenly, bang, back to reality with an abrupt epiphany: "Got to put *Puppy Chow* on the grocery list!" Now that's more like a human brain.

Even logical thinking—the kind you might expect from a rocket scientist or a McKinsey strategist—is more like a swallow wafting in the evening air, doing loop-de-loops and acrobatic tumbles, than an arrow sent shivering into a tree. We can't help it. That's the way the brain works.

For that reason, the human brain is also a lousy computer. And it's not one that you would probably care to employ. Can you imagine having a handheld calculator that begins humming "Strawberry Fields Forever" in the middle of a calculation? Or an ABS brake sensor that wonders, just as you are going into a skid, what it must be like to be an air bag deployer?

What characterizes human thought? "A period of mulling," says University of Chicago professor Howard Margolis, "followed by periods of recapitulation, in which we describe to ourselves what seems to have gone on during the mulling."[1] In other words, just like a swallow, the human mind thinks in a series of loop-de-loops.

But we haven't gathered here today to badmouth the brain. Quite the contrary. The brain is capable of doing marvelous things —things that computers couldn't imagine doing (if they could imagine doing anything). The appreciation of beauty, creativity, contemplation, imagination, and, yes, purple cows—these are all in the realm of the human brain.

When we talk about the creation of a thinking machine, in fact, this is the kind of intelligence we mean: not merely a machine that can calculate a sum to the billionth decimal point but one that has a sense of reason, balance, and intuition. A machine that can learn from its mistakes, as humans sometimes can, and even move the ball of civilization forward. Can we really build something like this, ever? This is an important question, but before we can answer it, we must ask ourselves, What do we mean by *thinking*? What do we mean by *conscious thought*? To answer those questions, I need to introduce you to Dan Dennett, my former philosophy professor and mentor.[2]

Daniel Dennett looks like what one might imagine a wizard would: part Oz, part Merlin. Like Hollywood's version, he has a shiny pate, bushy arched eyebrows, an immense mustache, and a beard that wiggles when he speaks. His crinkled eyes laugh with him when he exhibits his frequent dry wit. You would expect Dennett to be found in a cluttered office in an ivory tower institution, and in this respect he does not disappoint. Dennett spends much of his time in an office at Tufts University. But his personality, and his life, is much more multidimensional than that.

Dennett also sails his own forty-two-foot yacht. He's an excellent jazz pianist (who has played many a bar). He's also an expert downhill skier, a sculptor, and a tennis champion. His father was a Harvard PhD who worked for the OSS (and later the CIA) during World War II. The elder Dennett was killed in an airplane crash on a secret mission in Ethiopia in 1947, when Dan was five.

Dennett can speak brilliantly on many topics, but his greatest skill is in explaining what is meant by human intelligence. It was Dennett, in fact, who posed the purple and yellow cow question in his best-selling book, *Consciousness Explained*, and then explained the conundrum:

> "The trouble is that since these cows are just imagined cows, rather than real cows, or painted pictures of cows on canvas, or cow shapes on a color TV screen, it is hard to see what could be purple in the first instance and yellow in the second . . . Nothing roughly cow shaped in your brain (or in your eyeball) turns purple in one case and yellow in the other, and even if it did, this would not be much help, since it's pitch black inside your skull, and, besides, you haven't any eyes in there to see colors with."[3]

Beyond wondering how the images got there in the first place, Dennett takes the question one step farther. *Who* is it looking at those cows, anyhow? Who is the audience? Is there someone in the brain? Says Dennett, "The problem with brains is that when you look into them, you discover that nobody's home. No part of the brain is the thinker that does the thinking or the feeler that does the feeling."[4]

So if a thought is not in the brain, nor is the audience, where is it? What is thinking all about? And how in the world can we build a machine to replicate what seems inexplicable?

Dennett's answer is that there is nothing magical about the brain—no particular place where thoughts are created, as though in Santa's workshop. The brain is merely a wrinkled mass of carbon molecules, with the consistency of chilled butter, that somehow creates thoughts, reason, and emotion.

Because there's nothing magical in the brain, it means that there is no reason we cannot create similar functionality—such as thought, reason, and emotion—in a thinking machine made of, say, clay or silicon. After all, just as there is no particular reason for this lump in our heads to appreciate fine wines and music, daydream, and aspire to greater things, there is no reason that silicon or some other fundamental substance (maybe even carbon someday) could not be coaxed into creating something similar. Because the brain is nothing special in terms of materials—only carbon molecules—it is reasonable to assume that we can also build a machine with carbon (or silicon) that replicates its functions.

But what characteristics of thought should we aspire to in this artificial brain? The answer is that any machine we create must have the same loopy, iterative process as is found in the brain.

In other words, we need to create a machine that stops calculating from time to time to gaze out the window. We don't need the Amazing Hulk of supercomputers to do that. Dennett maintains that it can be done when "fixed, predesigned programs, running along railroad tracks with a few branch points, depending on the data, have been replaced by flexible, indeed volatile systems whose subsequent behavior is much more a function of the complex interactions between what the system is currently encountering and what it has encountered in the past."[5] Yes, we need a loop-de-loop.

Eric Clapton's Loop-de-Loop Machine

How did loopiness first arise in humans? Dennett believes it started when a single human—call her Eve—cried out, perhaps in pain. When no one responded to her, she did it again and again. And one day, the external cry became internalized. With humans, this first cry evolved into trains of thought—almost constant thought—that keep us thinking always, even when we are alone, sometimes to the extent that we talk to ourselves incessantly.[6] That, according to Dennett, is where consciousness, on the order of "I think, therefore I am," came from. In other words, like a swallow wafting in the wind, doing loop-de-loops, thoughts traveled from brain to mouth to ear, to brain, round and round, until internal consciousness arose.

That thought is echoed in *I Am a Strange Loop*, a stunning book by Pulitzer Prize–winning brain scientist Douglas Hofstadter. In the book, he argues that consciousness is an endlessly changing loop, where the brain is constantly fed information and constantly edits it, in an existence that is as elusive and self-repeating as the image we see of ourselves in a hall of mirrors.[7]

This is also, not coincidentally, how humans learn. "We human beings have used our plasticity not only to learn, but to learn how to learn better," Dennett says.[8] Yet another endless loop-de-loop. We repeat and repeat and repeat something until we get it down better and better and better. In his recent autobiography, guitarist Eric Clapton wrote, "I'd listen carefully to the recording of whatever song I was working on, then copy it and copy it till I could match it. I remember trying to imitate the bell-like tone achieved by Muddy Waters on his song "Honey Bee" . . . I had no technique, of course; I just spent hours mimicking it."[9] This is the primary thesis behind Malcolm Gladwell's newest best-seller, *Outliers*, in which he argued that the greatest achievements of humankind have come, not from genius or luck, but from reiterative practice.

To create real intelligence, then, we must make it on the order of the human mind, constantly questioning, learning, yearning, and looping. Just as a river is richer for its meandering, so must the brain follow a recursive path, looping like a swallow and practicing like Clapton around and around, until it not only learns but also learns how to learn.

So how do we build an Eric Clapton machine? Oddly enough, if we could create a machine that guesses, fumbles, rounds off, and is not very good with numbers (no offense Eric), we may be closer to something that replicates the human mind. What else do we need? One that is recursive, that edits itself continuously, that creates all kinds of little changes, tests them against problems, and discards the losers. We want a machine that learns through repetition and that would rather be half-right than completely right (not only because half-right is faster but also because completely right is a mental railroad track, devoid of the opportunistic loop-de-loops of real thinking). In other words, we need a prediction machine.

How do we do *that*? For that answer, I must introduce you to another of my mentors, Jim Anderson, whom I first met when he was the chairman of the Cognitive Sciences department at Brown University.

A Brain in a Bottle

Jim Anderson is one of the world's great brain scientists. His particular talent is in his ability to take psychological functions, such as concept formation, reduce them to the biological level, and then model them with computers. He is uniquely qualified in this area, given that he has degrees in physics and physiology from MIT. Anderson is also a true Renaissance man, having been a professor at Brown of brain science, cognitive science, applied mathematics, neural sciences, psychology, and biological and medical sciences. Anderson, in other words, *is* a brain.

For that reason, when I first walked into his office in the fall of 1998, hoping against hope that he would accept me for Brown's doctoral program, I was nervous. There he was, a thoughtful-looking man behind thick glasses, surrounded by books and papers, with—I should have known it—a brain sitting on his desk. Not a toy brain or a plastic model, but a real brain in a bottle, listing slightly to one side in a sea of dark green formaldehyde.

At the time, I myself could hardly be considered a brain—and certainly not a brain scientist. I had studied under Dan Dennett, but that was all. However, I did have another experience that I hoped would play to my advantage.

In 1994, a few years after college, I responded to the inspirational urgings of my parents ("Get a job!") and landed a job with GTE (which, after a series of mergers, changed its name to Verizon). As the (very) Young Turk in the office, I was assigned to a thing called "the Internet," and a project called "SuperPages." Super-Pages turned out to be one of the first Internet search engines, a program that would search Verizon's yellow pages and help consumers find the phone numbers and addresses of the businesses they needed.

With each iteration of SuperPages, I began to see the connection between what I knew of the brain and what we were doing online. For example, how information was presented online directly affected how it was perceived and interpreted both by humans and by Internet software.[10] The more closely we modeled our efforts on the brain, I realized, the better SuperPages performed. Moreover, when I began to study the emergent Internet as a whole, I had trouble finding areas where there were not analogies to the brain. It finally dawned on me that if I wanted to build Internet companies, I needed to know everything I could about the brain.

When I discussed this idea with Dan Dennett, he replied that "the brain" meant science and technology—and not only philosophy and psychology. What I needed to study was brain science, he said, and the place for that was Brown University, in Providence, Rhode Island. With that, he wrote me a letter of recommendation, and I applied for the PhD program. And so here I was, standing in the doorway of the office of Jim Anderson, with (I figured) about three or four minutes to talk my way in.

The meeting didn't start well. Most of the other applicants had done years of brain research, and my application, in comparison, looked like a joke. But the fact that Dan Dennett had sent me probably kept Jim interested enough to humor me. He asked me a few questions about the science of the mind, of which I had apparently little knowledge, and then switched gears and asked me to tell him about the Internet.

So I took a breath.

"The Internet is a brain," I said.

Not "The Internet is *like* a brain." I said, "The Internet *is* a brain." It was the wildest card I had. In fact, it was the only card I had. I figured it would probably get me bounced out of his office. But there it was; I had said it.

Jim was busy taking notes (more likely, grading papers), but when I said that, he looked up. He began to speak, and with every word he became more excited. Jim talked about the brain, technology, and evolution, but mostly he talked about the fact that he had always believed that telecommunications had followed the path of the brain. For more than an hour he continued, virtually uninterrupted, except for my occasional nod and "uh-huh." He even showed me old lecture notes and slides linking the two. "It is a wonderful analogy," he said.

It was a bit later that I decided to get something else off my chest: I confessed that my real reason for applying to the program at Brown was to get a PhD not to go into teaching or do research but to start a company—many companies, in fact—that would apply brain science to the Internet.

Jim studied me across his cluttered desk. "You can join the program on one condition," he said at last.

"What's that?" I replied feebly.

"That when you start your company, you'll make me your first employee."

As they say, the rest is history. I did start a company, called Simpli.com, and Jim became one of the founders. Within a few months, we had hired a good chunk of the cognitive science department at Brown. We went on to develop search engine technology with George Miller, National Medal of Science winner from Princeton—technology that is now the basis for the advertising capabilities of numerous Internet firms.

Better still, we sold that company in March 2000, only weeks before the Internet bubble collapsed, for about $30 million.

Artificial Brains

If anyone is on the right path to making an artificial brain, it is Jim Anderson. And the way he is doing it follows closely Dennett's definition of intelligence. In other words, Anderson is building a loopy brain. It's loopy because Jim's approach doesn't work in a logical or serial manner (*this* plus *this* equals *this*). Rather, like the brain, it does a thing called *parallel processing,* in which lots of ideas loop around in our heads simultaneously. Parallel processing, in many ways, is the key to understanding and replicating intelligence.

One of the cornerstones of parallel processing is pattern recognition. As our brains incorporate information in parallel, they are constantly looking for patterns to use in making educated guesses as to which process is best. As a result, we are constantly creating patterns, filling in the blanks, and interpreting the world around us, as opposed to observing it independently. Take a look at figure 1-1, and try to avoid seeing the triangle that does not exist.

You can't, of course, because as parts of your brain take in the information, other parts fill in the blanks. Now look at figure 1-2, which shows three pillars, all identical in size.

FIGURE 1-1

Try not to see a triangle

FIGURE 1-2

Which pillar is the longest?

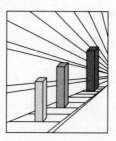

Most people do not believe that these pillars are the same size (they are), but they clearly see a group of columns cascading into the distance. In the real world, depth perception is a far more important visual cue than size. So this misperception is not necessarily a bad thing. We process the information in parallel, discard size, and focus on depth. Our survival, in many ways, has been dependent on allowing the most pertinent information to percolate to the forefront.

The brain has evolved to process almost everything in parallel, and this way of processing has enabled thought, foresight, and consciousness. The brain takes in information and then processes it. We do not do so in a linear series of "x, then y, then z" steps. Instead, our minds construct theories that compete with one another. Our one brain, it turns out, is really a multicomputational system.

As Anderson has noted, "One system is old, highly evolved, highly optimized, basically associative, perceptually oriented, memory driven, and logical." The second is "recent, oddly contoured, unreliable, symbolic and rule based."[11] In other words, the first system is very much like a computer; the latter, as you will see, is more like the Internet.

It is that second system—the cerebral cortex—that brings us human intelligence. So the human mind has billions of neurons working together in parallel, allowing us to walk, chew gum, speak, and remember someone's name, all at the same time. This is also how we will build real intelligence into the Internet. The only way to create the loopiness and iterative nature of the human mind, after all, is to emulate this quality.

With this, we can chip away at the mystery of human intelligence. Just as the microbe hunters of the past peered into their microscopes to reveal the secrets of organisms responsible for everything from smallpox to yellow fever, so can today's neuron hunters harness the power of the Internet to study the secrets of the mind.

Artificial Brains, Real Intelligence

I recently stopped by the Ersatz Brain Project at Brown, which, as the name implies, is focused on building a "fake brain." My favorite neuron hunter, Jim Anderson, was there. On his desk this time was not a human brain in a bottle, but a computer screen. Anderson and his colleagues were writing software that modeled neural networks.[12] At some point they will feed this software into the school's parallel processing supercomputer. And from that they hope some signs of intelligence, even at a primitive level, may appear.

As I watched, Anderson's programmers were building "minicolumns" of synthetic neurons. Minicolumns, composed of 80 to 100 "neurons" each, are the basic unit of the cerebral cortex. The human cortex, by the twenty-sixth week of gestation, is composed of a large number of these minicolumns, all set in parallel vertical arrays.[13] Of course, the brain has a lot of them—at least 10 to the 10th power of neurons, connected together with at least 10 to the 14th power of neural connections. In the brain, these mini-columns form clusters that bind together to form horizontal connections, or what Jim eloquently calls a "network of networks" (see figure 1-3).

In the brain, neurons work by switching themselves on and off. You might think of this process as black and white, but when you put a lot of neurons together and some are black and others are white, the overall expression becomes a certain shade of gray. We can do the same thing with computer chips. They are based on 1's and 0's. That's our black and white. But to imitate networks of neurons, we can also shave the 1's and 0's into finer slices—say, 0.1 or 0.06—and thereby get shades of gray similar to those of the brain. That's what Anderson's team is hoping to do.

FIGURE 1-3

Network of networks modular architecture

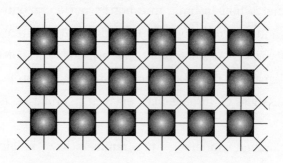

Source: Courtesy of James Anderson.

Anderson admits that he's starting small. His goal, he says, is to build a "shoddy, second-rate" brain. But if it can be built small, he can snap on additional components. It's like working with Legos. The more Legos you put together, the more patterns begin to form. When you snap together different patterns simultaneously, a new pattern forms. This is how the mind works.

In fact, Anderson says that a massively parallel computer—replicating the human cortex—is now technically feasible. It will require about "a million simple CPUs and a terabyte of memory for connection between the CPUs."[14] In the end, Anderson hopes to have shaped an intelligence that is an "adequate approximation of reality." For him that means it is "good enough." But good enough is far beyond the capabilities of computers. Good enough would combine speech recognition, object recognition, face recognition, motor control, complex memory functions, and information processing.

Anderson is working on groundbreaking theory and application. But if we are looking for a second-rate brain, it is already being built on a massive scale. What is the world's biggest parallel architecture—composed of millions of computers connected to one another? The Internet.

Imagine if the Internet were used to process information rather than merely pass it along. Well, it is being done by some of the biggest companies in the world.

Let's move on to the Pacific Northwest and take a look.

CHAPTER 2

Darwin's Cloud

CRUISING UP THE awe-inspiring Columbia River, with the cliffs rising steeply from its sandy banks and the many waterfalls twisting like white rope as they tumble from the cliffs, a visitor cannot help feeling the raw magnificence of nature. That sense is not diminished when you see the salmon pushing upriver, thrashing their tails as they force their way to their spawning grounds; nor is it diminished when you see, in a parallel sense, the many windsurfers on the river soaring and flipping against the wind-whipped whitecaps. This is life on the edge of something elemental—a struggle *against* nature and at the same time *of* nature—stripped clean so that it can be seen clearly and in full.

It is also here, at a town just up the river called The Dalles, that one finds a mysterious building rising among the barren landscape.

The building, as long as two football fields and with four cooling towers rising above, is surrounded by a tall barbed-wire fence. When construction commenced, the citizens of The Dalles learned that the complex was being built by Internet search giant Google—but little more. Rumors swirled after it was learned that the IT manager at the nearby Orchard View Farms cherry grove had been absorbed into the complex, along with several other locals—and grew stronger when none of the new Google employees, who had signed confidentiality agreements, would describe what they had seen inside or what they did there.

With questions mounting, Google finally invited a reporter and editor from *The Dalles Chronicle* to look around. More accustomed to reporting on the Chinook run, the walleye catch, and the bingo game at The Dalles Senior Center than on the shrouded activities of a corporate giant, the reporters found themselves being escorted past a high fence bearing a sign with a single word of warning: "Voldemort." That referred to the Harry Potter character known as "He who must not be named." Gulp.

What Google had billed as a tour, though, was little more than a snow job. The reporters saw nothing beyond the security building and the cafeteria. They were left to report that the Google buffet included barbecued pork, strip steaks, teriyaki chicken, vegetables, salads, and desserts. Red Bull and flavored iced teas were complimentary. Outside the cafeteria, Super Soakers were available should workers care to engage in an impromptu water-gun fight. Then plant manager Ken Patchett appeared and described how much he enjoyed fishing and hiking in the region and how glad his family was to be living in The Dalles. After that, the reporters were escorted out the gate.[1]

Had they been taken deeper into the heart of the building, however, this is what they would have likely seen: thousands of personal computers, none more powerful than the top-of-the-line desktop computer at Best Buy, wired together in metal cases, perhaps forty or fifty PCs to a case—the heat from their processors floating heavily above, rising up to the four cooling towers. They would have seen gray power cables and blue and orange Ethernet cables snaking through the building, connecting the PCs whose needs were being served by a hundred or so IT workers, their ears protected from the din of the whirring fans by noise-dampening earmuffs. If you picture the scene in the movie *The Matrix* when underground fields of humans were shown being harvested, you have the right image, although you must swap computers for humans.

In truth, the location of the Google complex at The Dalles has little to do with the quality of the local fishing and hiking. The complex absorbs massive quantities of electricity, courtesy of the nearby Dalles Dam, a 1.8-gigawatt power station that formerly powered an aluminum smelting plant, now abandoned. The dam produces enough power each day to launch a NASA shuttle into space. The second reason Google is here is the proximity of the 640-Gbps trans-Pacific fiber optic artery that runs from nearby Harbour Pointe, Washington, under the ocean to Asia. By tapping in to the artery, Google's computers can communicate with the world.

Computing in the Clouds

Why the secrecy? Part of the answer has to do with competitive advantage. In wiring together thousands of ordinary PCs, Google has created a supercomputer from small parts. The Dalles *server farm* (also called a *multiprocessor farm*) was Google's—and likely the world's—most advanced effort in parallel computing:

using multiple computers to simultaneously perform multiple tasks. The Dalles seems to be Google's most advanced effort, but it isn't the only one: Google has two dozen server farms scattered around the nation. And even though the details are a closely guarded secret, the total number of servers is likely more than half a million, with something like 200 petabytes of hard disk storage and 4 petabytes of RAM available. Keep in mind that with a single petabyte, roughly 1,000,000,000,000,000 (one quadrillion) bytes, your iPod could hold more than a million songs.

By bringing its server farms together in one big computing effort, Google has created *cloud computing*, in which massive computing power is coaxed from thousands of inexpensive PCs in a feat of massive parallel engineering. The point is not only that computing power can be made cheaper this way but also that it is faster to pull information from the RAM of ordinary computers than from the thick and dense disk drive of a single supercomputer.[2]

Cloud computing at Google got its start with the work of Christophe Bisciglia, a twenty-seven-year-old computer engineer, who not only had the idea of connecting multiple PCs to work in parallel (others had suggested it) but also got the system to work. From childhood, Bisciglia had all the markings of eccentric genius. He didn't utter a word for his first two years. Then one day when his mother was driving the car with Christophe in the backseat and the windows down, she heard from him his first communication: "Mommy, there's something artificial in my mouth."[3]

Fast-forward twenty-five years. Google had already invented MapReduce, a proprietary software that divided individual tasks into hundreds and thousands of tasks, assigned them to legions of computers, and then reconstituted the answer in nanoseconds. Now Bisciglia went to Google CEO Eric Schmidt with the idea of using the generic version of MapReduce to build a big computer from smaller PCs. He was given Schmidt's blessing.

Next, IBM CEO Sam Palmisano pledged support, and—with forty PCs hooked together —the experiment began. That was in 2006. Now Google has half a million PCs in parallel. Estimates have it, in fact, that the companies that are independently building cloud computing farms (including Google, IBM, Microsoft, Yahoo!, and Amazon.com) now have more than two million PCs humming together. These machines consume as much electricity as Las Vegas does on a lizard-scorching summer day, and the only challenge is finding more (cheap) electricity to consume. It is no coincidence that China is talking about building a series of nuclear power plants, and the cloud computing community—though it won't say so—can't wait.

Where will it all go? Mark Dean, head of research at IBM in Almaden, California, has said that the Internet will be getting a lot bigger with cloud computing coming on. "The web is tiny," he said. "We'll be laughing at how small the web is."[4]

For me, an equally important quotation comes from *BusinessWeek:* "When individual pieces [of a computing cloud] die, usually after three years, they are removed and replaced with newer, faster components. This means that the cloud regenerates its growth, *almost like a living thing* [emphasis added]."[5]

Selfish Software

The *BusinessWeek* statement is important because it picks up on the fact that we are enabling a technological *evolution.* People often talk about the history of technology. But what really is unfolding?

In Chicago's great Museum of Science and Industry, you can see a stunning display of steam locomotives, one following another, each faster and more efficient than the one before. Or visit the wonderful San Diego Air & Space Museum, where you can see the progress of planes, each better than the preceding ones. You can buy books on the progress of technology and wall charts that depict its development. But at some point you have to ask yourself, Is this forward march of technology merely happenstance, or is there something more behind it? To this question, quite a few people believe that the history of technology is really not a history; it is an evolution in the Darwinian sense—*a technological* evolution.

People have played around with this concept for years, in various guises. Benjamin Franklin remarked that "man is a tool-making animal."[6] In the mid-1800s there was great pride, a sense of "manifest destiny," as U.S. steamships and locomotives pushed to the far corners of the world. Eventually the concept encompassed a sense of national pride in Americans' general inventiveness and progress, as exemplified by the arrival of electricity, the automobile, and the airplane. Every industrialized nation has had its moments when this idea of progress steered its history.

But why? Theories were floated, but except for the idea that progress was good, the question was left to hang. Instead of worrying about the source of progress, economic thinkers used their talents to suggest how to channel it. Adam Smith suggested slicing and dicing productivity into manageable units—hence mass production and the foundation of the industrial age. Alfred Sloan came along and (with Pierre du Pont and eventually Peter Drucker) advanced those ideas into the twentieth-century model of organizational management.

This theory of management involved the invention of the notions of hierarchy and individual accountability, along with the creation of divisions, which together led to the conglomerate. General Motors, GE, U.S. Steel, and Standard Oil Company were the leading standard-bearers of this new organizational model. With the advent of computing, technology, and the Internet, information became more accessible to everyone in an organization. Subsequently, many thinkers have developed new ideas for shaping an organization and stimulating creativity and innovation within the corporate walls.

But little was heard about the origins of innovation until 1976, and then it came in a cannon blast from an unexpected source: not from the pundits of technology, nor from business, but from the formaldehyde-drenched halls of biology. In that year, a young Oxford scientist named Richard Dawkins proposed that Darwin had told only part of the story of evolution. Darwin had said that evolution involved changes at the species level, where mutation and natural selection led the most "fit" (and adaptable) to succeed.

But Dawkins's big idea was that natural selection actually starts much deeper, at the level of genes, which battle it out to determine which of them will survive to the next generation. Species evolve, in other words, but so, too, do genes.

Dawkins's theory led to the book *The Selfish Gene*, which has sold more than a million copies in twenty-five languages.[7] Dawkins immediately drew fire from strict Darwinians, who disputed his theory, and from Creationists, who damned its message as one of cold atheism. Whenever you are reviled by both sides in a debate, you know you have a big idea on your hands.

Dawkins had another surprise waiting. The second big idea is that "selfish genes" are not the only thing driving all living things onward. There are also *selfish memes.* What are selfish memes? Dawkins said a *meme* is a "unit of culture" that is transmitted by imitation and naturally selected by its popularity or longevity. A meme is a thought or idea, then, one that evolves and propagates through natural selection.

Dawkins classified memes as "tunes, ideas, catch phrases, clothes, fashions, ways of making pots or building arches." Mythologies, folk songs, fashions, and knowledge—such as how to start a fire, forge iron, make a pot, and even how to build an automobile or a light bulb factory—are all the product of selfish memes. He noted, "Just as genes propagate themselves via sperm or eggs, so do memes propagate themselves in the meme pool by leaping from brain to brain via a process which, in the broad sense, could be called imitation."[8]

If ideas evolve, leaping from one person and one generation to another, is it a stretch to believe that technology could likewise evolve? Call it "selfish software." This is similar to what French anthropologist André Leroi-Gourhan has called the "freeing of tools," as tools are envisioned in the imaginations of the inventors before they are "freed" to materialize on the workbench.[9]

To be sure, technology doesn't always go forward in a linear fashion. When less-advanced technologies compete by being more efficient, by being cheaper, or by opening new markets, the march of technology frequently takes the shape of an S curve (as noted in the book *The Innovator's Dilemma*).[10] But neither is biological evolution uniformly upward (in fact, Darwin wrote a note reminding himself not to term particular evolutionary changes "good" or "bad"). In both cases, it is not about progress but about the march of evolution.[11]

Could it be, then, that the selfish gene became frustrated with the slow evolution of the human brain (we haven't had a decent biological advance in about fifty thousand years) and so leapt the fence from the organic world to the inorganic? Could selfish genes have created selfish memes to do their work? And is that what has led us to selfish software? Is that why humankind, imprisoned as we are in carbon molecules, is driven to invent machines made of sand and metal? I'm not completely convinced. But when you consider the history of technology as the evolution of technology, the perspective is exhilarating.

Cracking the Digital Code

All this is particularly interesting when you look at computers, because computer software and genetics are not dissimilar. In fact, Dawkins has said of the genetic code that it is "truly digital, in exactly the same sense as computer codes. This is not some vague analogy, it is the literal truth."[12] So it is worth understanding how we were able to replicate the genetic code.

The history of the thinking machine started in 1832 with Charles Babbage's mechanical computer: a seventeen-ton assemblage of wooden gears, cranked by hand, that for the first time replicated the one-step-at-a-time logic of humans—who were, at the time, called "computers." (Note that companies back then, particularly shipping concerns, called the people whom they employed to do math and basic calculations "computers," and Babbage's invention was designed to replace them.) Next, Babbage laid plans for a machine that could perform simple logic: IF such and such, THEN this would happen. As he envisioned it, the computer would be ten feet high, ten feet wide, five feet deep and driven by steam. It was never built, and Babbage died without realizing his dream.

Fast-forward one hundred years to 1936 and to a theory by Alan Turing, a British mathematician who postulated that any process could be described as a computation, driven by 0's and 1's, which is the underlying assumption behind modern computers. Turing's ideas, as neuroscientist Reed Montague puts it succinctly, "went two big steps beyond Darwin's. First, Turing's ideas transform Darwin's discovery into a computation—they portray evolution itself as an algorithm: Vary, select, retain, or discard." Moreover, Turing's ideas "unite life, mind and machine."[13]

Because life runs on algorithms, minds run on algorithms. And we know that machines run on algorithms, so they are all fundamentally the same. (If you built a Tinkertoy model of this thought, you'd have a Ritz cracker–sized wooden block in the middle as the processor, and three wooden spokes—life (evolution), the mind, and machines—all plugging in to the round block.)

Turing's idea was revolutionary. "To the extent that the world obeys mathematical equations that can be solved step by step, a machine can be built that simulates the world and makes predictions about it," notes Harvard psychologist Steven Pinker. "To the extent that thought consists of 'apply any set of well-specified rules,' a machine can be built that, in some sense, thinks."[14]

Other Turing computers followed. In 1940, a computer called Robinson successfully decoded messages from Enigma, the German enciphering machine. In 1943, an even more powerful computer called Colossus was used by British scientists to decode German messages. In 1944, the Mark 1 computer used punched paper tape for programming.

Then, in 1945, John von Neumann published a paper describing in detail how to build what is close to the modern computer (the EDVAC). It combined the two essentials of modern computing: stored programs and memory. It was, furthermore, a machine that worked through hundreds and thousands of 0's and 1's ("bits" of information) divided into "words" of 8, 16, 32, and 64 bits. What is interesting about von Neumann's proposal for this machine was not only how often he described its functions in terms of human behavior (memory) but also how he specifically compared its functions to that of the neuron—the fundamental switching device that routes electricity around the brain.[15]

Since von Neumann, the computing industry has only gained steam. Gordon Moore, the cofounder of Intel, is famous for noting that for the past twenty years, computing speeds have doubled about every eighteen months. Meanwhile, costs have declined at an inverse rate. As author and inventor Ray Kurzweil noted, if the automobile had evolved at the same clip, a car today would cost a hundredth of a penny and go faster than the speed of light.[16]

Back to The Dalles

I remember pondering the speed of this evolution as I stood at the edge of the Columbia River during a 2005 visit, watching the salmon fight their way up the steps of a human-made fish ladder. The thrashing, relentless drive in our species to create intelligence is of that kind—not even a rational drive but an unfathomably elemental compulsion, one that matches the force of evolution itself.

Where is our thrashing upstream journey taking us? I like the way George Gilder said it in a recent issue of *Wired*: "The next wave of evolution will compress today's parallel solutions into an evolutionary convergence of electronics and optics . . . With that, the petascale computer will shrink from a dinosaur to a teleputer, the successor to today's handhelds in your ear or your signal path . . . moreover it will link to trillions of sensors around the globe, giving it a constant knowledge of the physical state of the world."[17]

This next wave of evolution is already under way. The parallel processing computing clouds are transplanting the functionality of the ordinary computer. We are moving from an individual computer to a networked one. Google, Microsoft, Amazon.com, Yahoo!, and others are opening up their clouds to other businesses so that companies can start using the computing power in place of their own PCs and servers. One of my companies—Web.com—has almost 300,000 small businesses leveraging our cloud. Millions of companies are giving up their centralized solutions in favor of rented space in a cloud.

Computing in the Clouds

This brings us back to Google's cloud. Why is the computing complex shrouded in secrecy? Why the ominous warning from Harry Potter? Why are Google's engineers and brain scientists forbidden to speak a word of what they do under the Google roof? To be sure, part of it has to do with the Google cloud being a big brawny computer—a supercomputer. That is certainly an accomplishment. But there is much more to the secrecy than that.

The fact is that Google and the other cloud makers hope that their parallel computing clouds can create some semblance of human-like intelligence. In other words, their quest for better distributed computing is the same quest as that of neuron hunter Jim Anderson and his Ersatz Brain group. The goal: create the loopy, iterative stuff of the human mind.

Google's effort is spearheaded by MapReduce, a simple, powerful software program that enables automatic parallelization and distribution of large-scale computations. In other words, it allows Google to use the cloud and the Internet to think in parallel.

MapReduce does what our brains do: it categorizes (maps) key pieces of information, distributes them across its server farm of PCs, and then eliminates (reduces) irrelevant data; in contrast, computers—unlike MapReduce and the brain—soak in everything. And MapReduce does all this without the rigidity of the traditional computer (as one Google senior vice president recently boasted, "Nobody builds servers as unreliable as we do").[18] Google now uses MapReduce for more than ten thousand programs, ranging from the processing of satellite imagery and large-scale machine learning problems to language processing and responding to popular queries. Each day it processes roughly 100,000 functions and digests 20 petabytes of data.[19]

As the inventors of MapReduce noted in a recent paper, "It has been used across a wide range of domains within Google including: large-scale machine learning problems; clustering problems . . . ; extracting data to produce reports of popular queries; extracting properties of Web pages for new experiments and products . . . ; processing of satellite imagery data; language model processing for statistical machine translation; and large-scale graph computation."[20] In other words, the tasks Google performs are similar to the functions performed by the brain: learning, categorization, vision, and language.

This range of tasks opens the door to the analysis of vast amounts of information—from petabytes of data on the voting habits of Americans, from the fluctuations of billions of individual airline fares to scores of petabytes of health data. "The biggest challenge of the Petabyte Age won't be storing all the data," *Wired* noted recently, "but figuring out how to make sense of it."[21] Making sense of it: that is where Internet intelligence is now heading.

The Internet as a Computing Cloud

What does the Internet have to do with cloud computing? The Internet is a cloud—a cloud of computers hooked together, communicating. It typically is not used for computing, but there is nothing to stop us from using the entire Internet as a massive computing cloud.[22] If you put together the Internet and cloud computing, you have an integrated machine that does the three things most important to the brain: information storage, processing, and communication.

When the clouds of processing and the clouds of communication merge, and when they perform on parallel levels in the haphazard, loopy way of the brain, human-like intelligence will likely spread across the Internet. As Google CEO Eric Schmidt pointed out in 2003, years before he joined Google, "When the network becomes as fast as the processor, the computer hollows out and spreads across the network."[23] This is where all the information on the Internet must be crumpled like our paper model of the brain; where patterns must be established, where multiple drafts live and die, so that intelligence is created.

In a recent *New York Times* article, Bill Gates acknowledged that the pace of technology—as it drives toward intelligence—is as relentless as the fighting salmon migrating upstream. "They did MapReduce," he said of Google's efforts. "But we have this thing called Dryad that's better." He paused and then conceded the inevitability of something stronger and fitter: "But they'll do one that's better."[24]

The evolutionary imperative, this time courtesy of Bill Gates.

PART II

Internet Intelligence

CHAPTER 3

A Wise Guess

G AVIN POTTER IS NEITHER a computer scientist nor a programmer. Yet Potter is the front-runner in one of the hottest computer programming contests of recent times.

The contest was organized by online movie rental company Netflix. The company has a technology, called Cinematch, that helps customers find good flicks. How? Netflix uses fancy algorithmic gymnastics to match a customer's previous selections against thousands of other possible films. (Netflix calls this "straightforward statistical linear modeling, with a lot of data conditioning.")[1] Netflix can even recommend the perfect "movie for two," something that, considering the Venus-Mars tastes of many couples, should be considered a minor miracle.

But Cinematch has one big problem: its algorithm tends to rec-ommend best-sellers (because success begets more success) to the point that less popular films—those that might really please a par-ticular viewer—are ignored. What to do? Netflix called on its cus-tomers for help. In fact, it offered a million dollars to anyone who could improve Cinematch's film suggestion process by at least 10 percent.

With that, the Netflix Prize was born. Within months after its announcement, some twenty-five thousand teams and individuals applied for the Netflix Prize. Most of them were computer and math whizzes. By October 2007 (the end of the first year of the competition), a group of Princeton alums had achieved second place with a program that was 8 percent better. A team from AT&T was in first place, with an 8.43 percent improvement over the Netflix formula. Both teams used complex algorithms to better the formula. Still, none had achieved the 10 percent improvement necessary to win the million bucks.

But then Gavin Potter arrived on the scene. His first attempt improved the Netflix algorithm by 7.15 percent; his sec-ond, 8 percent; his third attempt, less than a month later, gained 8.07 percent; and by October 2008, he was approaching 8.79 per-cent. Who was this guy? It took a reporter from *Wired* to track him down. He turned out to be a forty-eight-year-old retired consultant with an undergraduate degree in psychology from Oxford who was working out of a bedroom office near London. When asked why he joined the quest, he replied that it looked like fun. And "being an unemployed psychologist means that I do have a bit of time," he said.[2]

What value could a psychologist bring to a computer science conundrum? Plenty, it turns out, because the answer to Netflix's problem—predicting what someone may like—has a lot more to do with the way the human brain works than with shaping an algorithm to satisfy a computer.

We may not be able to predict the weather next week, but in many other ways, the brain is an excellent prediction machine. Early humans, for instance, didn't need to see their prey to know that an animal was ahead. They could predict its progress by observing its paw prints and droppings. In fact, without being able to forecast the imminent future, early humans would have been consumed by whatever beast was lying in wait in the bushes ahead.

That brings us to a related marvel of the brain: intuition. Without intuition, the human race would have been finished a long time ago. Intuition rests on the ability of the brain to read patterns and react accordingly. For instance, you don't need to accumulate hundreds of details about a coiled object in your path to jump out of the way. The brain instantly intuits that it's a snake. Now the object may merely have been a coiled rope—and you may have jumped into the air needlessly, only to amuse your friends hiding behind the bushes. But that is because the brain is built to react quickly. It doesn't wait for all the details. In fact, having too many details can bog down the brain. That's right: *too much* information is bad. It can actually cause a kind of mind-freeze. Find that hard to believe? Consider the story of Ben Franklin's nephew.

One day, Benjamin Franklin realized that his favorite nephew was unable to choose between two pretty girls to marry. Sensibly, Franklin advised the young man to make a double-columned list, with the attributes of one girl on the left and the other on the right. Then, said Franklin, the young man need only cross out the attributes that were equal in weight, and the girl with the most attributes remaining would be the one to wed.

The young man made his list, crossed out the equal attributes—and then realized that the girl he really loved (and would marry) was the one with the fewest attributes. So much for Uncle Ben. This wonderful story, told by Gerd Gigerenzer in *Gut Feelings*, makes a profound point: intuitions based on one good reason are often more accurate than conclusions drawn from extensive studies based on reams of data.[3]

How does this story relate to Netflix? In the Netflix case, most of the teams vying for the prize were building algorithms based on crunching more data than did the original Netflix formula. But Potter had the opposite idea. He built his solution on *less* information—only a few films that quantified the tastes of the viewer, rather than all of them. As with the brain, because Potter's solution was simpler, the calculations were much faster.

At this writing, Potter has yet to achieve the 10 percent improvement required to win the prize (nor has anyone else). But the lesson is clear: the brain is intelligent not because of the sheer volume of data it can ingest, but for the way it can quickly discern patterns—and then guess. That's what makes the brain something that we don't always associate it with: a prediction machine.

Mental Levitation

In *The Wisdom Paradox*, neuroscientist Elkhonon Goldberg describes the process that we often call enlightenment, epiphany, or the Eureka moment: "As I am trying to solve a thorny problem, a seemingly distant association often pops up like a deus ex machina, unrelated at first glance but in the end offering a marvelously effective solution to the problem at hand. Things that in the past were separate now reveal their connection. This, too, happens effortlessly, by itself, while I experience myself more as a passive recipient of a mental windfall than as a active straining agent of my mental life." Goldberg calls this windfall wisdom, and he finds that as he ages—to his delight—he has more of it than when he was young. "What I have lost with age in my capacity for hard mental work, I seem to have gained in my capacity for instantaneous, almost unfairly easy insight." Indeed, it is wisdom, that "mental levitation."[4]

This benefit is derived not because Goldberg's mind is a calculating machine, but because the mind has developed associations, memories, and a *mechanism of anticipation* that raises the total beyond the sum of its parts.

Wisdom is not an out-of-the-brain phenomenon. It's not, as Goldberg says, "hovering over our heads like a saint's halo."[5] It is instead a product of the brain. From that sticky three-pound ball comes the ability to shift our eyes rapidly and leap before a rattlesnake strikes. From it we can decide quickly on the particulars of a shopping trip—a feat that would keep a computer grinding away for years. To top it off, from the brain we can derive wisdom, the nearly magical ability to solve problems and pass judgment.

Part of the reason for these gifts is an apparent weakness of the brain: our shoddy memory system. As I said earlier, the brain is an inefficient machine. It's expensive to maintain memories, and so most of them fade quickly. The brain is also slow. Transmissions to the cerebral cortex range from one to thirty meters per second along the axons, and about one-third of a meter per second along dendrites. Compared with the transmission speed of a computer or fiber optic network (light travels at about 300 million meters per second), the brain is a slacker. Moreover, the time it takes for a neuron to snap on and off in your head is about two-thousandths of a second (one-thousandth of a second if you are really quick). A computer does it a million times faster. Finally, neurons fire at about twenty to one hundred times per second (OK, technically they can get up to several hundred pulses per second, but then they drop back exhausted). This speed pales in comparison to that of the standard transistor in your laptop.[6]

Taken together, these weaknesses explain why we humans must try to keep predicting what will happen. Call it guessing or intuition, but the brain teaches us to do it by rewarding our correct guesses. It does this by distributing little spurts of dopamine (the same substance that is overproduced when an addict uses an illicit drug like heroin) throughout the brain. (Along each side of the brain stem we have about twenty thousand dopamine neurons, which have sent out long axons throughout the brain.) The desire for these dopamine fixes coaxes out smart guessing.

Suppose you have a piece of chocolate in front of you. Based on experience, your brain predicts that it will taste good, and your hand reaches for it and drops it into your mouth. The next step is even more important: forget the piece of chocolate. Just mention the word *Godiva*, and you get a similar biological reaction. Pavlov's dogs had nothing on us humans.

Or how about emotionally laden concepts, such as freedom of speech? Or higher taxes? Motherhood? Apple pie? For many of these concepts, the brain's reaction is preconfigured (for better or worse) based on experience. The pattern is set. A *value* has been placed on the thing. Therefore, the brain doesn't have to do any fresh thinking. It has predicted its reaction.

"All brains are, in essence," Dan Dennett tells us, "*anticipation* machines."[7] That is the primary thing we need our brains for. It is not the only thing, but the brain is far too expensive a resource to be of evolutionary benefit otherwise. Disagree? Consider the juvenile sea squirt, which frets about life until it finds a safe haven in the fissure of a rock. "When it finds its spot and takes root," says Dennett, "it doesn't need its brain anymore, so it eats it (it's rather like getting tenure)."[8] Brains are too expensive (and nutritious) to let them go to waste.

We humans use anticipation every day. Think about what happens when you look out at the world. When you spin a cup of coffee around so that the handle has moved from the left to the right side, your mind doesn't go about reexamining the entire cup. It doesn't need to start from scratch. It knows from previous experience that the mug of coffee is the same. It just fills in the change in the handle.[9] Similarly, when we step out the front door in the morning, our brains pretty well know what to expect. Memory serves us well. The patterns are there. If you step out of your front door in the morning and find a dead body on your sidewalk, that would be something to note. But you needn't examine the oak tree in the front yard as though it had never existed before.

What's interesting about this is that Plato, in his famous "Theory of Forms," stated that a perfect tree, a perfect flower, a perfect model of everything exists in the ether of the heavens. For centuries, philosophers have explored the meaning of this statement. Now, brain science offers new enlightenment: our brains do hold perfect representations of things—memory patterns (such as the scene that greets your eyes as you open your front door)—that can be quickly and cheaply called upon. To that prototypical image, the brain merely makes a quick comparison, noting whatever is new. These memory patterns, of course, are predictions—preemptive expectations of what we will see. They are, in the words of Harvard psychologist Steven Pinker, "the internal simulation of possible behaviors and their anticipated consequences."[10]

Future Shock

To figure out what to do, the brain must gaze into the future. It must imagine things. It must simulate possible future scenarios. Furthermore, the brain must also evaluate those scenarios to determine which are most likely. And then, to save energy (so that it doesn't have to do them repeatedly), it must *learn* from those simulations. And always the thought must come around to one framed not in the past, not in the present, but in the future tense: "Now what do I do?"

Forward thinking is the brain's way to chip away at the edges of uncertainty, to make bets based on experience. Furthermore, the human brain is good at learning not only what did happen but also what *didn't* happen. We are able to make, as Pinker terms it, "fallible guesses from fragmentary information."[11]

Many predictions are driven by the *amygdala*, an almond-shaped cluster of interconnected structures perched above the brain stem near the bottom of the limbic ring. The amygdala is the seat, not of reason, but of passion and emotion. But it also plays a role in predictions. In fact, in times of crisis, the amygdala can spring into action before the rationally thinking *neocortex* has time to make a level-headed decision.[12]

Think again about the rattlesnake in your path: the visual signal goes from the retina to the thalamus. The *visual cortex* gets the first pass at the coiled object, analyzing what the shape means. Then it passes the information to the neocortex for further processing. That makes sense. But recently, researchers have noted that part of the response goes directly from the thalamus to the amygdala, circumventing the neocortex (parallel processing in action). Because the amygdala can house memories, those memories can make us respond—even though we don't know why. We don't analyze the slithering object on the ground; we jump.

"While the hippocampus remembers the dry facts, the amygdala retains the emotional flavor that goes with those facts—that means that the brain has two memory systems, one for ordinary facts and one for emotionally charged ones," writes Daniel Goleman. "Just as there is a steady murmur of background thoughts in the mind, there is a constant emotional hum."[13] What's interesting is that unlike other parts of our brains, the amygdala is fully formed at birth. Obviously, it was deemed crucial enough for survival to merit priority.

So we have a brain that sees patterns rather than individual pixels of information; a brain that uses stored knowledge to anticipate things; and a brain that has intuition. And for baby boomers, the really good news is that with time, it only gets better. Sure, the neurons in the brain die, but our wisdom expands.

The brain, because of its weaknesses, is a marvelous thinking machine. It can arrive at answers through intuition that "no conceivable search engine, running for the lifetime of the universe, could hope even to scratch the surface of."[14] This is precisely why Gavin Potter had an advantage over the computer scientists in tackling the Netflix challenge: as a psychologist he looked for the human answer, not the one that would have been offered by a machine.

Logical Flaws

Conventional wisdom would have us believe that clear, rational thought is the basis of human intelligence. Aren't we taught the power of categorical propositions such as, "All clowns are funny; some clowns are sad people; therefore, the prediction: some sad people are funny"? Venn diagrams (known especially to consultants and business strategists) are common ways to express such logic. And then you have Boolean algebra (named after English mathematician George Boole), which can express these relationships in the language of math. Boolean algebra, in fact, is what drives computers. It allows them to calculate and to solve problems.

But if you want a machine that has *human* intelligence, that isn't the way to do it. Imagine that you are playing chess the way a computer must play. It has been calculated that there are not 20, or 50, or 150, or even 3,000 possible moves in a game of chess. There are 10 to the 120th power possible moves—1 followed by 120 zeros. As James Hogan explains it, that sum far exceeds the number of atoms in the universe.[15]

But let's think of something less taxing than chess. How about taking a simple trip around town to run errands? Suppose you need to make ten stops: the bank, the gas station, the post office, the dry cleaners, four electronics stores (to compare prices), and two clothing stores. Do you know, logically, the possible number of combinations of stops? You have 3.6 million options. Adding only one more stop would push the possible combinations of where to go next to 40 million choices.[16]

Sure, the human brain could calculate all 40 million options before you went shopping, but how long would you be standing at the kitchen table before you went out the door? Trying each option would be the equivalent of opening a combination lock by trying every possible combination. Or finding John Smith in New York City by starting at one end of Manhattan and stopping everyone you encountered until you reached the other side. That's not how the human brain works.

In fact, imagine the brain calculations going on in the outfield as your everyday Little Leaguer tries to catch a ball: you have the ball's distance, its initial velocity, projection angle, ball spin, air resistance, and wind turbulence, not to mention the uneven terrain in left field—and any other thoughts migrating through the outfielder's mind (pizza, girls, texting)—to contend with and possibly gum up the works. How in the world can the brain make all these calculations simultaneously and speedily? There is no assemblage of computers—not even the hundreds of thousands of computers linked in parallel in a thunder cloud of mechanical intelligence—that could maneuver the mitt to capture that sphere of torn horsehide.

Gambling with Uncertainty

The brain is good at making predictions, but it is not flawless. As I said earlier, the coiled object in our path might not be a snake after all. So we jumped in the air for nothing. What's interesting is that some of our other perceptions are equally wrong. Alexander Pope said, "To err is human." But it is also human to deny that we err. Let me give you an example.

When I was sixteen, along with a few of my friends I decided we could make money playing blackjack. I was convinced at the time that we had an unbeatable system. We knew that it was highly unlikely that we would lose multiple times in a row, so we pooled all our money (enough to play about ten hands) and set out to beat the house. My friends and I ended up at Foxwoods Casino, the largest casino in the world and, at the time, the most lenient for underage gambling because it was located on an Indian reservation. Our plan was simple: bet $10 every time you win, and double the bet whenever you lose.

For a while we did very well, but eventually the laws of statistics caught up to us. What we failed to realize was that just because you have lost nine times in a row does not mean you are more likely to win the next time. If we had done a bit of research, we would have learned that our system had been proven disastrous many times by researchers and gamblers alike (it even has a name: the gambler's fallacy), but we were not the brightest bunch of sixteen-year-olds. I felt vindicated years later when I asked Brown University students far brighter than me a similar research question: a coin is tossed in the air nine times, and it lands heads every time; what is the likelihood it will land tails on the tenth flip? Few of the students thought the answer was 50/50.[17]

My mistake (and the student's bias) is symptomatic of an overall problem with our brains: they were designed to make educated guesses, but that design causes systematic mistakes. We are all *predictably irrational*, as Dan Ariely contends in a recent book. Our brains are great at what they do because they work so well in imperfect situations—but that also makes us vulnerable to errors in judgment.[18] At no time is this more pronounced than when we try to forecast the future. This is one of the reasons Nassim Taleb argues in *The Black Swan* that we are guilty of ascribing far too much predictability to the truly unpredictable. He goes so far as to say that even the success of Google was based largely on random luck.[19]

Back to the Future

If the brain is so good at predictions, why are we so bad at forecasting? A number of scholars have noted that our ability to make forecasts—whether of hurricanes lashing the East Coast of the

United States, the incidence of AIDS in Africa, long-run blackjack odds, or the number of deaths accountable to secondhand smoke— fails regularly because the prognosticators make the same mistakes repeatedly: they use averages that don't depict real events. Forecasters essentially take complex natural phenomena and "model" them (poorly) in the lab. And of course, they make the big mistake of assuming linearity, even though nature is linear only until it's not. (If linear extrapolation really predicted the future, notes biologist Stephen Jay Gould, then we could predict that the Boston marathon—which is being run in faster and faster times—will eventually crown a champion at 0 minutes and 0 seconds.)[20]

Hindsight makes forecasting appear even less accurate, almost comical. For that reason it is rare to see a futuristic account in books or movies that isn't judged in retrospect as being widely off the mark. Steven Spielberg did a great job when he produced the movie *Back to the Future*, in which the heroes travel in time from the 1980s to the 1950s. And Spielberg succeeded as well in *Back to the Future III*, when his heroes went back to the 1800s. It was *Back to the Future II* that was the bomb; Spielberg had to look forward from 1985 to 2015 for that segment, and his vision failed to target many of the "futuristic" aspects of contemporary life (such as cell phones, iPods, the Internet, and laser eye surgery) but instead depicted clichéd flying cars and the like (hey, it was only a movie!). But most of us (unless we are Leonardo da Vinci or Nostradamus) are no better at tagging the future.

That said, there is a difference between forecasting and predicting. Forecasting is about making long-range predictions. But the brain makes everyday predictions, the kind that help us walk and talk and think and play baseball. These predictions happen in milliseconds and cover a time span of a few seconds. Call them mini-predictions, but that is what makes the brain tick. Predicting where a ball will land so that you can place your mitt in that vicinity is something the brain is good at; predicting who will win the next pennant is forecasting, and we are terrible at that. And guess what: computers are the opposite. But that is now changing on the Internet.

How do we replicate the prediction capabilities of the mind? That effort has been under way since 1947, beginning in the hands of a young economist (and future Nobel Laureate) named Herbert Simon.

CHAPTER 4

Too Much
of a Good Thing

INFORMATION OVERLOAD—too much data—was a problem of particular interest to a young man named Herbert Simon. Simon was a business expert who had helped administer the Marshall Plan and in 1947 wrote a book about operations research called *Administrative Behavior*.[1] In 1978, Simon won the Nobel Prize in economics for demonstrating that economics has as much to do with the brain as it does with math. He spent the rest of his life trying to build a computer that could think like a brain. There wasn't as much theory then about how the brain works, but Simon instinctively realized that people don't make decisions by weighing every possible alternative. They simply don't have the time. So they make "good enough" decisions based on what has worked before.[2]

In 1952, while Simon was working as a consultant for the Rand Corporation in Santa Monica, California, he met Allen Newell, a graduate in physics from Stanford. Newell felt the same way as Simon about what would later be called artificial intelligence. In 1955 they left Rand for the Carnegie Institute to develop a computer program that would exhibit human intelligence.

That program, they realized, had to be based on the way the brain works: the brain, rather than being a precision instrument, runs on rules of thumb. It remembers experience, shapes it into patterns, and then uses the patterns to guess what's coming down the pike. These guesses could be called hunches or intuitions. But the name that has stuck in the scientific world is *heuristics*, a term coined by mathematician George Pólya, who had been Newell's tutor at Stanford. Heuristics are the rules of thumb (based on experience) that whittle our choices down to manageable numbers, such as deciding to group the stops on a shopping trip so that we first go to all the electronics stores to make price comparisons while they are fresh in our minds.

To test this theory, Newell and Simon wrote an algorithm having certain heuristics and fed it into their computer. What would have taken the computer tens of thousands of years to compute if it were making one calculation after another (like checking each person in New York City one at a time) was instead completed in one-fourth of a second.

In June 1956, Newell and Simon presented their work at a conference at Dartmouth College. It was the first time that anything approaching "human" intelligence was coaxed out of a machine. John McCarthy, the assistant professor at Dartmouth who had organized the meeting, termed it *artificial intelligence* (AI), and the name stuck. Before long, researchers were adding other touches of common sense to their algorithms—manipulations such as generalizations, associations, pattern similarities, analogies, and maxims. This practice became known as *fuzzy logic*.

In July 1979, at the Winter Sports Palace in Monte Carlo, these efforts reached a high-watermark of sorts. Here, Luigi Villa, an Italian backgammon whiz, had just been crowned world backgammon champion. But he stuck around for one more contest. As the theme from *Star Wars* blared from the speakers, a three-foot-tall robot emerged on stage, tangled itself momentarily in the curtains (causing the cheering crowd to burst into laughter), bumped into a table (evoking more laughter), and then took its place across a backgammon board from Villa. The robot, dubbed Gammonoid, was connected (via satellite) to a computer located at Carnegie Mellon University in Pittsburgh.[3]

The computer program had been written by Hans Berliner, a world correspondence chess champion and student of Herb Simon's. When the audience settled down, the game commenced. No world champion, in any board game, had ever been defeated by a software program. But Berliner had carefully shaped the heuristics in the program along the lines of human thinking. He didn't tell Gammonoid *how* to win; he didn't tell it *what* to do in every circumstance. If he had, Gammonoid would have spent years making those step-by-step calculations until he toppled over in a smoking heap. Rather, Berliner wrote the software to predict patterns that would pare down the possible alternatives, much as the brain does. Six games were played, and in each one Gammonoid beat the world champion. The world was amazed (and rather amused) by the feat.

"Gammonoid the Conqueror," the *Washington Post* exclaimed the following day.[4]

Did Gammonoid possess human intelligence? No. He could do one thing: play backgammon. He couldn't even chew a stick of gum, let alone decide to do so. And that was the problem in trying to build a prediction machine like the mind. But that was OK with Simon. Gammonoid was only the beginning. "It is not my aim to surprise or shock you," he said, "but the simplest way I can summarize is to say that there are now in the world machines that think, that learn and that create. Moreover, their ability to do these things is going to increase rapidly until—in a visible future—the range of problems they can handle will be coextensive with the range to which the human mind has been applied."[5]

Gammonoid was replaced by Deep Blue, the IBM computer that in 1997 beat world chess champion Gary Kasparov. That triumph, as great as it may have seemed, was similar to Gammonoid's. It didn't prove that a robot had human intelligence. In fact, it provoked brain scientist and author Marvin Minsky to note, "Deep Blue might be able to win at chess, but it wouldn't know to come in from the rain."[6] In a sense, Gammonoid and Deep Blue hampered the quest for the thinking machine, because they instilled the idea of "artificial" intelligence among us. What we want, really, is an artificial thing that creates real intelligence. To get that, we need to make something that can tackle predictions, heuristics, and intuition, as Simon demonstrated years ago.

The Flaw of Information

We tend to assume that the best way to solve a problem is to have perfect information and perfect calculation. But it is prediction in the face of limited information that makes our brains, well, thoughtful. In *Blink: The Power of Thinking Without Thinking*, author Malcolm Gladwell relates a situation in which prediction triumphs. Gladwell tells the story of the victory of Confederate General Robert E. Lee over Union General Joe Hooker at the battle of Chancellorsville. Hooker had the upper hand: a larger army that had been divided so that it was squeezing the Confederates in a vise. He also had infiltrated Lee's army with spies and had an abundance of information.[7]

But Lee sensed what Hooker was up to, and so he divided his army and quietly sent his forces into place near the Union encampment. When Hooker's men were eating dinner, the Rebel forces descended on them, sending the Union soldiers into a rout. "It was wisdom that someone acquires after a lifetime of learning and watching and doing," Gladwell explains. "It's judgment . . . Lee's ability to sense Hooker's indecision, to act on the spur of the moment, to conjure up a battle plan that would take Hooker by surprise—his ability, in other words, to move quickly and instinctively on the field of battle—was so critical that it is what made it possible for him to defeat an army twice the size of his. Judgment matters: it is what separates winners from losers."[8] In short, Lee took advantage of his ability to predict.

Gerd Gigerenzer, who has authored numerous academic articles on prediction, offers another counterintuitive idea.[9] According to Gigerenzer, intuition often arises from how *little* we know of something rather than how much. He notes, "Intuitions based on only *one good reason* tend to be accurate when one has to predict the future (or some unknown present state of affairs), when the future is difficult to foresee, and when one has only limited information." In other words, he says, one good reason is better than many. Less is more. And with that one good reason, notes Gigerenzer, we can get "almost unfairly easy insight."[10]

In the case of Hooker and Lee, Hooker had the advantage in facts. He had a network of spies, and he had hot air balloons floating nearly over the Confederates' heads. He was dead sure of himself. "My battle plans are perfect," he boasted. "And when I start to carry them out, may God have mercy on Bobby Lee, for I shall have none."[11] Bobby Lee didn't have the same wealth of information; in fact, he was so blissfully in the dark that Hooker managed to move seventy thousand Union troops behind him without his knowledge.

What caused General Lee to prevail? According to Gladwell, Lee had the *blink mojo* working for him—the instinct to react fast, move swiftly, and push the element of surprise back on Hooker. Or, as Gigerenzer would argue, Lee had just enough information and nothing more. Lee didn't need spies and hot air balloons circling the battlefield; he had patterns in his head that predicted the path to take. In World War II, Dwight Eisenhower could be said to have done the same thing: faced with the complexities of D-Day, with the weather deteriorating and the bold invasion of Europe possibly already detected, he made a decision with limited information, and the decision was to go.

We see this kind of decision making play out every day. Some executives become victims of analysis paralysis, thinking they need to weigh every bit of information against all possible outcomes. Those executives rarely make it very far. In contrast, other executives make quick decisions, based on limited information, using the brain's implicit ability to predict the best path.

Monty Hall and Door Number 3

Have you ever heard of the Monty Hall Dilemma? This is a behavioral science experiment derived from the game show *Let's*

Make a Deal (whose host was Monty Hall). In the experiment, "Monty" asks the subject to choose between three doors: one hiding a new car, and the others hiding gag prizes. Once the subject has made the decision (say, door number 1), Monty opens one of the unchosen doors (let's say door number 2) to reveal a gag prize. It is now clear that the car is behind either door number 1 or door number 3. Then comes the dilemma: Monty asks the subject, "Do you want to stay with the original door you chose, or switch?" What would you do?

Most people choose to stay with their original choice. But that is the wrong decision. In fact, you are two-thirds more likely to win the car if you switch. Why do people make the wrong decision? It turns out that Monty Hall is giving people *too much information*, the kind of information that Gigerenzer and Gladwell were concerned about. The right decision would have been much easier if, after you chose door number 1, Monty offered you the choice to switch and keep doors 2 and 3. In that case, everyone would switch, as we demonstrated in research studies while I was at Brown. But the two scenarios are actually identical.[12]

How about this brainteaser, courtesy of Amos Tversky and Nobel Laureate Daniel Kahneman: "'Linda' is 31 years old, single, outspoken, and very bright. She majored in philosophy. As a student she was deeply concerned with such issues as discrimination and social justice. She also participated in several anti-nuclear demonstrations. Now, is Linda more likely to be a *bank teller* or a *feminist bank teller*?"[13]

As Tversky and Kahneman's research has shown, most people say Linda is more likely to be a feminist bank teller. But why? Linda is always "more likely" to be a bank teller, because the category "bank teller" is larger than its subcategory "feminist bank teller"; it is irrelevant whether or not she is feminist. This is an example of information overload, one where information (her college major, her concerns, her political actions) causes errors in judgment. Gigerenzer showed that part of the problem stems from how information is presented.[14] And with a group of colleagues from Brown, my team showed that decisions could be reversed by reducing the amount of information or even spacing it out appropriately.[15] With *less* information, we more easily attain the right answer.

Companies haven't yet gotten to the point of limiting people's access to data, but I suspect they will. The most recent trends are to increase information flow, build larger data warehouses, and spend more time analyzing before making decisions. These practices go counter to the wisdom of the brain and the insight behind *Blink*. Gladwell's book is in fact one of a minority of books about decision making. Most are focused on increasing information flow and driving more data into the decision process. More-sophisticated tools are being brought to market—not to simplify things, but to increase the complexity of data. But that is the wrong model for business. It is also the wrong model for a prediction machine.

Making the Internet a Prediction Machine

Amazon.com's prediction system is as sophisticated as they come, precisely because it discards data in favor of pattern recognition. Think about the last time you were presented with a book suggestion from Amazon.com (hopefully this book). My mom recently purchased a book on Amazon.com after reading a recommended suggestion. The suggestion was so insightful and yet so out of left field that she was convinced a human was behind it. Why are the results often so good? It was Amazon.com's strong predictive algorithms at work—algorithms that substitute human-like decision making based on a few pieces of data rather than an overwhelming amount. It was by no accident that this happened: Dan Ariely, my MIT mentor and author of the best-seller *Predictably Irrational*, helped Amazon.com build some of these intelligent algorithms.[16]

Steven Johnson, author of *Emergence* and *Mind Wide Open*, also cites Amazon.com's prediction capability: "The recommendation agent that we interact with at Amazon has gotten remarkably smart in a remarkably short time," he writes. "If you've built up a long purchase history with Amazon, you'll tend to get pretty sophisticated recommendations . . . The software doesn't know what it's like to read a book, or what you feel like when you read a particular book. All it knows is that people who bought this book also bought these other ones; or that people who rated these books highly also rated these books highly . . . Out of that elemental data something more nuanced can emerge."[17]

These algorithms work by looking for patterns in how we buy, rate, and recommend books. From this data, patterns emerge that may, as my mom said, come from left field but are incredibly powerful. As Amazon.com founder Jeff Bezos puts it, "I remember one of the first times this struck me. The main book on the page was on Zen. There were other suggestions for Zen books, and in the middle of those was a book on how to have a clutter-free desk."[18] He goes on to say that this is not something a human would do.

But this is exactly the type of association a human would make, and that is what makes it powerful. Amazon.com was able to make the link between a Zen book, past behavior, and the fact that Bezos was looking to clean up his desk, just as a colleague in human resources might do after peering through a stack of papers, only to find a hapless boss feverishly reading a book on Zen.

At Simpli.com, we built a prediction engine (developed in part by Jim Anderson and Dan Ariely) that let us compare user searches to advertising. If the user had searched at some point for chips and snacks (versus chips and Intel), the technology would target the user with, say, a Pringles ad. This is similar to the technology that Google now uses for AdSense, its advertising system.

Using this same technology at NetZero and Juno, we would present people with ads after they visited particular sites. So you would receive a Pringles ad after you visited, say, P&G.com, Lays.com, and KidsSnacks.com. Later we leveraged other useful information: user search terms, click stream data, and buying patterns (see figure 4-1). We increased our most valuable inventory while offering narrower targeting for advertisers.

FIGURE 4-1

Prediction engine at Simpli.com

User click-through: Procter & Gamble Web site
User Profile Interests: Snack Foods > Potato Chips

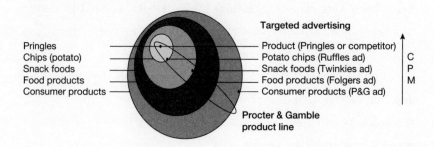

Pringles
Chips (potato)
Snack foods
Food products
Consumer products

Targeted advertising

Product (Pringles or competitor)
Potato chips (Ruffles ad)
Snack foods (Twinkies ad)
Food products (Folgers ad)
Consumer products (P&G ad)

C
P
M

Procter & Gamble
product line

The nice thing about running an ISP is that you have endless amounts of data. But as you have seen, prediction is more about eliminating data than using it. So our model identified the universe of possible opportunities and cut it to a narrow set of targeted ad spots. With so much ad inventory on the Internet, reducing the amount available can actually drive revenues higher. So when users' behavior indicated they might like Pringles, we matched them directly to a Pringles ad; if users were of a broader mind or undecided, we would open up the inventory and give them a more general treat—maybe Pringles, maybe Twinkies, maybe both. And the benefits to the advertisers were striking: more clicks, higher sales, and an overall increase in the efficiency of their marketing programs.

Predictions based on limited information, as you can see, are essential to the operation of both the brain and the Internet. But another consideration is in play: in both the brain and the Internet, thoughts and ideas come and go. They are created and destroyed. And the brain has created an interesting way to deal with this deficiency. Don't believe me? Turn the page. I predict that the next chapter will reveal it all.

CHAPTER 5

Creative Destruction

O N WEDNESDAY, August 18, 1965, Brad Williams ordered a hamburger at the Red Barn restaurant— an experience he remembers with pinpoint accuracy. That might not seem extraordinary, except that Williams was eight years old then and now, at fifty-two, has no particular reason for remembering it. The fact is, Williams remembers almost every detail about his past. What happened on November 7, 1991? Williams replies, "It was a Thursday, a big snowfall had hit a week before . . . and Magic Johnson had announced [a few days earlier] that he was infected with HIV."[1]

Most people don't have that kind of memory. Our thoughts work more like this: you are driving and hear an advertisement on the radio. It gives a phone number to call. Recognizing that you don't have a pen or paper handy—let alone your trusty Black-Berry—you hasten homeward, repeating the number under your breath. Heaven forbid that another thought enters your mind! You get home and jot down the number. And then, like a little demon struggling to be free, the number flees your mind.

So what's up with human memory? Unlike a computer's memory system, the human memory system is not infallible. In fact, human memory is more like a garden fountain. The little cup at the top fills, spills the water down to the next cup, then to the next cup, and then down the drain.

"Thank God for that," states neuropsychologist Elkhonon Goldberg, noting that otherwise, our brains would be clogged with useless information.[2] Indeed, photographic memory might sound like an exciting gift, the kind of superpower that Superman might possess. But before you make it one of your three wishes, think about its implications: one woman in her forties—with an even greater memory than Williams—recently said her memories nearly drive her mad. It's "nonstop, uncontrollable and exhausting," she has said. "I run my entire life through my head every day, and it drives me crazy."[3]

Indeed, for most of us, old thoughts are replaced instantly with new ones. "A new memory begins forming the moment you encounter whatever it is you are learning: a new face, a new fact, or a new sound," says Goldberg. "New proteins are being synthesized, new synapses are developing, and other synapses are being strengthened relative to the surrounding synapses."[4] It's the abbreviated memory that makes the human brain a creative, remarkably resilient thing. Tossing out the old thoughts and bringing in the flow of new memories built on new perceptions and experiences—these processes are the real source of human intelligence.[5]

If we begin to look at memory in general, then, what we see is a constant ebb and flow of cutting-edge memories, each building upon the others, ranging from the time and date when you last ate a hamburger (a memory that may last a few days) to how much you enjoyed your last vacation (a memory that may last a few years). For the most part, memory is a process that could be called *creative destruction*. Your mind creates a thought; important thoughts remain; unimportant thoughts exit. Every day, that's what happens.

So creative destruction is how the brain works. The constant refreshing of the mind is what leads to creativity and new ideas. More importantly, it leads to the constant reediting of life. If we didn't have this process, we could never think of anything new. We'd be in a brain freeze. And obviously, evolution recognized that being in a brain freeze is not a good place to be.

Most people think of economics when they think of creative destruction, but it is not only about free markets. It is how the brain works, how companies are built to last, and how the Internet has been unfolding. In our never-ending quest to build bigger, better products on the Internet, we often miss the true meaning of creative destruction: less is more. Just as the brain forgets as much as it learns, the companies that succeed are often slower, less nimble, and imperfect; but just like the brain, they get the job done. Companies that succeed leverage creative destruction to build disruptive products, services, technologies, and advertisements.

The Business of Creative Destruction

Outside the philosophical tomes of Nietzsche, the concept of creative destruction was first popularized by Joseph Alois Schumpeter in his 1940s book, *The Theory of Economic Development*.[6] The essence of Schumpeter's argument was that the theories of most earlier economists advocated systems that ran forever—within companies that were built to last, not through flexibility but hard-nosed resilience. Schumpeter criticized John Maynard Keynes and Adam Smith, because their ideas about capitalism suggested an equilibrium between supply and demand that offered hope of an economic perpetual motion machine. In the 1940s, when companies were truly built to last (at least the mightiest of them), the idea of creative destruction was foreign to much corporate experience. But Schumpeter believed in the "gales of creative destruction," a constant sweeping out of the old by the new.

As big business changed in the 1990s, with the rusting and collapse of the industrial age and the rise of the "new economy," creative destruction described what was happening. In *The Innovator's Dilemma*, Clayton Christensen pushed the idea even further, noting that it's not only the better and faster companies that dominate over time; sometimes a company can kill its bigger competitor by doing something *less* well.[7] He wrote, "Occasionally disruptive technologies emerge—innovations that result in worse product performance, at least in the near term . . . generally disruptive technologies underperform established products in mainstream markets. But they have other features . . . they are typically cheaper, simpler, smaller, and frequently, more convenient to use."[8] *Rational innovations*, on the other hand, are linear improvements, the kind of incremental innovations that over time become too cumbersome and finally sink companies.

Any study of evolution will show that nature can overshoot itself; witness the lumbering dinosaurs, heavily plated with armor, versus the weaker (but soon dominant) mammals. What better metaphor for the big company is there than a beast that can't see around its own girth to the upstarts nibbling at the grass below? This is the big idea behind *The Innovator's Dilemma*—that the march of technology is not on an upward curve but rather a series of S curves.

I'm not sure Christensen ever connected his big idea to this statement from Darwin: "There is a frequently recurring struggle for existence, and it follows that any being, if it varies however slightly in any manner profitable to itself under the complex conditions of life, will have a better chance of surviving, and thus be naturally selected." Or as Stephen Jay Gould eloquently explained in *Full House*, "Evolution, to us, is a linear series of creatures getting bigger, fancier, or at least better adapted to local environments . . . [but] natural selection talks only about adaptation to changing local environments . . . no feature of such local adaptation should yield any expectation of general progress." Gould adds that written in Darwin's personal journal were the words, "Never say higher or lower." Darwin could just as well have said that the process of evolution is a case study in creative destruction.[9]

In some cases, creative destruction leads to a situation in which "bigger is better" (a process that eventually killed the dinosaurs); sometimes we conclude that "smarter is better" (although that notion may kill humankind, as was the belief during the cold war); but just as often, creative destruction is a matter of déjà vu all over again: "cheaper is better" (like my trusty Timex) or "older is better" (the QWERTY keyboard). And with the acceleration of the Internet, we seem to be closer than ever before to replicating this cycle of regressing to progress.

Creative Destruction on Madison Avenue

The speed at which creative destruction affects Internet businesses probably is not nearly as great as it is within the advertising industry. For the past fifty or so years, marketing was pretty much a one-trick pony. Ogilvy, Mather, Young, Rubicam, Saatchi (and Saatchi), and all the rest built their reputations on creating great advertising campaigns. The adage of the past was, "Understand consumers, appeal to them, and get them to buy." In the era of advertising, brands mattered most.

But with fast feedback and direct marketing, that model is changing. To be sure, the model changed years ago with the advent of direct-response advertising through the mail, TV infomercials, and the Home Shopping Network. But the Internet provides a greater wealth of feedback, more inventory than other media, and response times measured in milliseconds, not days.

Consider, as an example, The Search Agency, which was started a mere six years ago and has already become one of the largest online advertising firms. Among more than one hundred employees, none of them is a traditional marketer.[10] Why? It's because, in the online world of fast media, a marketing background often can be counterproductive. With the ability to track changes in real time, you no longer need to think through the best way to advertise; instead, you throw everything you've got into the universe and see what works. This is creative destruction at its fastest, most frenzied pace.

For a typical search marketing campaign on Google—for, say, a *Fortune* 500 company or a top 10 Web site—The Search Agency may test as many as ten thousand keywords, one thousand different pieces of copy, hundreds of pictures, and numerous variations of Web sites. On top of that, it may have two dozen price points and a baker's dozen products and packages in rotation. Campaigns are measured in performance (determined by sales, visits, or whatever else the client determines as success) across multiple dimensions: time (to the second), geography, demographics, user profiles, and other data.

These campaigns are complex, but the model is simple. Imagine a campaign for Ford to test every variation of search words—*car, cars, auto, Ford Truck, GM* (yes, competitors' keywords tend to perform well)—and every combination of creative pitch: *buy Ford, buy Ford Trucks, Ford Trucks are cool, buy Ford Truckes* (yes, misspellings often perform well). Then you see what works best and when. For example, *Ford Trucks* performs best on the keywords *car* and *auto* between 8 and 10 p.m. for men in Green Bay; worse than *Ford Truckes* between 4 and 4:30 p.m. in Green Bay, but equally well in Seattle, for women during that time.

Imagine hundreds of thousands of variables and thousands of ad campaigns, all competing with one another to survive and flourish (and that's only for one Ford truck). Each set of campaigns is a new generation, pushing forward one step at a time. The whole process goes so fast that often we don't even know what is working or why. Internet ad campaigns evolve faster than fruit flies—and I wouldn't be surprised if there are more of them buzzing around the Internet at any one time than fruit flies on Earth.

How do we know which campaigns are best? It's simple: we let creative destruction, in the form of algorithms, create a model of survival of the fittest, in which only the best campaigns live to fight another day. The best of the bunch are pitted against a new campaign and are left to fend for themselves. Sound a bit maddening? It is, but that is creative destruction. No brands, no positioning, no marketing—only creative destruction at the speed of a parallel processing computing cloud.

The Internet Creatively Destructs

It's not only online advertising that creatively destructs, but also the entire Internet. Think back to the late 1980s, when the Internet was opened to the world by several Internet service providers (companies such as PSINet, UUNET, Netcom, and Portal Software). These ISPs provided expensive direct links into the Internet. Those companies were later eclipsed by narrowband ISPs that offered inexpensive (yet slower) access to the Internet through phone lines.

As you've seen in *The Innovator's Dilemma*, an inferior technology replaced a superior one—because the inferior one better addressed the needs of consumers. This is creative destruction. I saw it firsthand while working at United Online, which owned NetZero and Juno.[11] First, the company offered consumers a free ISP at a time when other internet service providers were charging $20 or more a month. This offer sent the market running toward NetZero and Juno. Then a *value split* was created by offering speeds as fast as AOL's but charging half the price. This cannibalized the market for free access, but it propelled the company to record growth and a billion-dollar stock.[12]

NetZero and Juno also used a trick that is essential to the brain: in this case, instead of using costly broadband connections, new technology called caching was utilized. *Caching* is the equivalent of short-term memory. The team's idea was to sidestep the permanent servers, where information resides, and instead create copies of content in places that users find easiest to reach. Essentially, the company identified the most popular content on the Internet—content that needs to be readily available (just as the brain has certain information that must remain "top of mind") and stored it in a short-term server farm, where it could be retrieved quickly and sent to users.[13] This short-term memory gave NetZero and Juno a competitive advantage. It was an inferior product compared with broadband. But like the brain, it was fast and easy—and good enough.

So the Internet is a case study in creative destruction. As we pursue a smarter Internet, the path is an S curve. It often takes one step back before it moves forward. Nowhere is this more pronounced than in the underlying fabric of the Net. Interestingly, Tim Berners-Lee is now proposing to rebuild his invention (the World Wide Web), creating a "semantic Web." He wants to create links and content containing information that can be understood by humans *and* by computers. This means tearing down the underlying code of the Web (HTML). The semantic Web will get us closer to real online intelligence.[14]

With Web 2.0, we have seen the emergence of mass collaboration, social networking, podcasting, wikis, blogs, and collective consciousness.[15] Web sites have become dynamic, and anyone with a computer as a mouthpiece can now impact the Web. As a result, thousands of companies that did not evolve imploded—companies such as AltaVista, AOL, and Netscape. But others, like eBay, Google, and Amazon.com, have adapted and thrived. And of course, the MySpaces, Facebooks, YouTubes, and Wikipedias were born.

Now we are taking all that even further. "I have a dream for the Web [in which computers] become capable of analyzing all the data on the Web—the content, links, and transactions between people and computers," Berners-Lee has noted. "A 'Semantic Web', which should make this possible, has yet to emerge, but when it does, the day-to-day mechanisms of trade, bureaucracy and our daily lives will be handled by machines talking to machines. The 'intelligent agents' people have touted for ages will finally materialize."[16] Many people, including Berners-Lee, are now calling this Web 3.0.

PART III

The Brain
Behind the Web

CHAPTER 6

A Web of Neurons

THE HARDWARE OF THE INTERNET is little more than a network of computers and phone lines. It is an incremental improvement over what came before. But the World Wide Web is a transformational change. It is more than improved wires and connections. It is the primordial soup from which I believe human-like intelligence—reasoning, intuition, and creativity—will one day arise.

The Web is a system of interlinked hypertext documents accessed via the Internet. Hypertext (developed at Brown University in the 1960s) appears most often as blue underlined text that you click on to open other Web sites, as though you were passing through a door into a new realm of content.[1] Using hypertext you can also post information, link it to other information, and share it around the world. A Web browser permits you to roam the Internet, searching for pages and videos that you might want to see.

What is particularly interesting about Web sites is how analogous they are to the web of neurons in the brain. Just as neural networks are the home of thoughts and memories in the brain, Web sites are the repository of content, thought, and memory on the Internet.

A Symphony of Lights

Each neuron in the brain has about 7,000 connections, for a total of some 100 trillion connections. These connections form neural networks, essentially hundreds of millions of neurons connected to one another. But these connections are not haphazard. They are made in a special way that allows the brain to form and recognize patterns. The design of this network of neurons is what makes the sparks happen. It creates another layer of complexity that we can think of as a semantic network. It is here that all our thoughts and memories are stored. If you think of the semantic networks as the software of the brain, and the neural networks as the hardware of the brain, you get the general picture.

How does it work? When you hear Beethoven's *Symphony No. 1 in C Major* or Elvis's "All Shook Up," your brain encodes the music across millions of neurons. (Imagine a Christmas tree blinking in a particular pattern for each tune; our "tree," of course, has 100 billion lights.) A neural network is like a well-orchestrated symphony of lights. When you hear the song again (or start humming it in the shower), those lights flash in that pattern again. The more these networks are triggered together, the stronger their connection becomes. That's why neuroscientists say that "cells that fire together, wire together."

These connections may also evoke emotions: the first time you heard "All Shook Up" you may have had pleasant thoughts that, in turn, released endorphins that made you smile. All that was encoded, so the next time you heard the song the neurons lit up in the same pattern, and you got the same emotional kick. That's why happiness and smiling go hand in hand; they happen so often together that they are like the proverbial horse and carriage (try to smile and not feel happy; it's hard to do). So the secret to happiness is surprisingly simple: if you're feeling down, smile. You will feel better.

Of Minds and Memes

What's the connection between the brain and Web sites? The brain has networks of neurons that form a semantic network of memories, and the Internet has a World Wide Web of Web sites.[2] Web sites are the software of the Internet, just as memories are the software of the mind.

What's interesting is that the Web is growing far faster than is the evolution of the human brain. Five million years ago, the brains of our evolutionary cousin, Australopithecus, weighed about 450 cubic centimeters, the same as that of the present-day gorilla. By 500,000 years ago, the brains of the Neanderthals had more than doubled in size to around 1,000 cc. More recently, the brains of Cro-Magnon grew 50 percent larger than that, or roughly equivalent to the modern human brain.[3]

That rate of growth may be fast, but it's nothing compared with the growth of the World Wide Web. In its first ten years, the Web grew by 850 percent per year. By 2008, there were about 175 million Web sites.[4] To be sure, it would have to grow much more to catch up with the brain's 100 billion neurons and 100 trillion connections, but the Web is on track to grow much faster than the human brain.

Yet we already have something approaching a semantic network online. Just as healthy neural networks create memory systems, the Internet enables the World Wide Web. Just as memories connect to related memories, Web sites connect to related Web sites. As a result, both the brain and the Internet are brimming with ideas, good and bad. In other words, Web sites are memes.

As I noted earlier, biologist Richard Dawkins defined memes as ideas that live, spread, and die just as genetic material does. For the most part, memes are driven by language. Our ability to communicate allows memes to spread, mutate, and grow.

The human brain evolved as a hardwired device until about 150,000 years ago, when it suddenly grew fourfold, creating the one-eighth-inch thick mantle that covers the earlier, primitive brain like a shower cap. It was this part of the brain, the cerebral cortex, that gave us language. It was at this stage that communication became an important part of evolution, and something remarkable happened: the mind began to outrace evolution. Rather than experiencing a radical improvement in the brain itself (the hardware), humankind began to develop software—cultural software—that has improved over time.

At the core of this process is the trading of ideas and the reaping of advantage in the trade—whether it be American Indians teaching pilgrims to place a fish in the hole (along with the seed) when they plant Indian maize, or latter-day medical Web sites and blogs passing information about diseases and cures around the world at blinding speed.

Dan Dennett, as always, describes this evolution in the most charming of ways: "Being able to speak is such a Good Trick that anyone who was slow off the mark getting there would be at a tremendous disadvantage. The first of our ancestors to speak almost certainly had a much more laborious time getting the hang of it, but we are the descendants of the virtuosos among them."[5] What Dennett is saying—and what Richard Dawkins was advocating—is that the evolution of memes is not merely analogous to genetic evolution; it is an *extension* of it. The evolution of memes is as significant to the evolution of the human species as was the opposable thumb—and as detrimental as cancer. Some memes can be beneficial to us, as in the social drive to quit smoking. Others, such as thoughts of suicide, are harmful.

Beneath the Surface of the Pond

That brings us back to the Internet, the great purveyor of memes, expanding in speed and density at an exponential rate. The average Web site, like the average idea, is seen only by the person who created it. Memes, it turns out, behave in a way that's very similar to the behavior of Web sites. Memes are competitive, fight for space and visibility, and often spam for attention (whether it is a credit card Web site or an annoying jingle that we can't get out of our heads). To compete, a good Web site must cater to its obvious and not-so-obvious audience: people and computers. Otherwise, it will disappear into the invisible sea of Web sites.

The Web is a seething, dangerous place for any aspiring meme. How does a Web site continue to create and propagate rather than destruct? As I said earlier, a Web site, like a meme, needs to transmit itself. And like memes, weak Web sites don't make the grade. In the brain, neurologists tell us that weak memories, ones that fail to resonate with many others, are constantly jettisoned for stronger ones.

The same can be said of Web sites. But you must remember who is looking at these sites, and this is where things get tricky. There are the usual suspects: moms, pops, kids, academics, and consumers alike. But let us not forget the other brains: spiders, bots, algorithms, smart agents, and the other creepy crawlers on the Web.

Search engines have been able to create *spiders* (or *web crawlers*) that creep around the Internet reading what's there. These agents are sent by numerous companies to retrieve information about the Web so that the sites can be indexed and categorized using intelligent algorithms. Google's algorithms, for instance, search for the Web sites with the greatest amount of meme-ness— sites that are rich in content—to feed the larger Internet brain. Other sites are put so far down in the Google search engine that they spend lonely lives and eventually die. As you can see, the Internet, like nature, is red in tooth and claw.

To survive, Web sites need to be novel and appealing. Me-too memes always die, and so do me-too Web sites. But the average Web site is a terrible meme machine. On the Internet it may actually be worse than in the brain, because you also must deal with myriad search engines. A Web site must be among the top few search results, or else it is irrelevant. Our brains can process only seven or so ideas at once, so if it is ever to be seen, a Web site must be displayed in the first page of a given search. If you search for "grizzly bear" on Google, it will return more than two million results. But most people don't go past the first page, so the millionth Web site might as well be about a "bear shitting in the woods."

If your site is not in the top seven to ten results (let alone the top million) in a search engine, it is not relevant. Yet millions of dollars are wasted every year trying to move Web sites from number 1200 to 400 to 40 in the Google rankings; it's a nice statistic to present to your board, but it will not increase sales. You would be much better off defining your category more narrowly rather than trying to move up the rankings in a broad category. Whether you are a Web site on the Internet, an idea in the mind, or a bully in the schoolyard, it is better to be a big fish in a small pond.

Web site survival, then, depends on finding a niche to dominate. A pizzeria in Des Moines, Iowa, cannot compete with Domino's, or even become Iowa's best pizzeria. It has no chance of becoming number 1 in Google's pizza category. But the site does have a great shot at becoming number 1 for pizza in Des Moines. Similarly, why should a Web site compete (and lose) in vintage sports memorabilia when it could instead narrow its niche and be the number 1 distributer of hardwood flooring from the old Boston Garden? For a site to be successful, it must be Hertz (number 1) and not Avis ("We try harder"). Remember Yoda's response to the Avis commercial: "Do or do not; there is no 'try.'"

Even if the content is right, an unreadable Web site exists on the edge of destruction. Like birds with the most lustrous feathers, Web sites must strut their stuff properly. Google's Web site is the right example: an uncluttered look, a few key links, and a nice big button for sending the information on. That's the paradigm for meme reproduction. On the other hand, Web sites that are complex and hard to navigate might as well give up, because they are set up for destruction. I always use my grandmother as the test of a site's readability. If she can figure it out, it is all good.

The Eyes Have It

I read recently that crabs, when they emerge from the water, cannot sniff the air for mates (as they do in the brine). So when crabs are on land, how do they find the right honey? Looks. Now

I don't know what turns on a crab (the legs?), but I do know that Web sites live and die according to how good they look to visitors. Attractive features include audio, graphics, text, even pop-ups versus pop-unders. You have a huge numbers of options. Some things prevail: people are inherently visual, for instance, so a picture can substitute for a thousand words. Text should be short, simple, and consistent.

Web sites can prevail simply by placing information wisely on the screen. Eye-tracking studies have been performed to evaluate what people look at first. An *eye-tracker* is a clunky device that is fitted to a person's head and tracks, you guessed it, eye movement. It turns out that our eyes are constantly moving, and eye-trackers identify what we are "really" looking at.

It surprises most people to learn that our eyes are constantly moving. It is yet another trick that the brain plays on us: we perceive that our eyes are looking directly at what we think we are seeing, but that is a fallacy. The brain is too slow to process information from our eyes at rates more than a few degrees across the retina per second, which happens whenever we are moving (and we are almost always moving). To compensate, our eyes move constantly as we look at things, a jerky movement called a *saccade*.

It is difficult for us to focus on moving objects, and they make for a good demonstration of our visual limitations. Take a look at a whirling electric fan. Once the fan blades start moving, turning into a blur, the individual blades are virtually indistinguishable. But it is not movement *per se* that causes the blur. If you turn off the fan and move your head as fast as you can while looking at the fan, the blades will become distinguishable because your eyes will remain focused on the blades by moving against your motion. As you read this book, the same thing happens. Although your body doesn't move much, your mind and interests do; thus, your eyes move in saccadic jerks to and from various spots on the page, occasionally stopping at certain points. Eye-trackers accurately track these eye movements.

Eye-trackers show that certain information is best presented in certain ways. For example, people tend to ignore text in favor of graphics. They also ignore large text in favor of smaller text. And they spend an inordinate amount of time looking at navigation bars, headers, and lists.[6] These tendencies may be an artifact of the ubiquitous banner ads of the early dot-com era. Those ads were so annoying that most people started ignoring anything that even remotely looked like an advertisement, such as graphics or big, bold text. A term was even coined for this tendency: *banner blindness.*[7]

A Spider's Web

But Web sites not only must play to the human audience but also must show the right stuff to the spidery algorithms sent into cyberspace to go exploring. These algorithms play by different rules. Although people as well as spiders start reading from the upper left (at least for languages that go from left to right), spiders tend to look for the biggest fonts, descriptions of graphics (people typically ignore these), metatags (people always ignore these), navigation bars, and other links. Crawling and indexing on Google alone take more than two hundred steps. (Of course, the human process is even more complex, given that we activate millions of neurons to perform the most mundane tasks, such as reading this book.) What is a Web site to do? The smart ones play by the rules that humans like. That's because most spiders try to replicate the way people look at sites so that they can provide results that are consistent with people's needs and interests.

But it is never that easy. The best Web sites have a consistent set of internal links, a navigation bar, and a site map or list of all of the pages. Spiders navigate the Web through links (they have no fingers to type URLs). Site maps make their lives easier. Imagine a restaurant critic who uses a wheelchair. She will probably give preference to restaurants that have wheelchair access, even if it has nothing to do with the food. Spiders have feelings, too: as a result, they have been programmed to give priority to sites that have maps and navigation bars.

The best Web sites also have a specific topic for each page, along with a representative keyword that is repeated often (but not too often). Spiders try to *categorize* the site. This means that they look for keywords or ways to reduce a site's long-winded (in their opinion) text into a single keyword. Smart Web sites stay alive by making the spiders' lives as easy as possible. They avoid having disparate information on a single page. A Web site for pizza in Des Moines, for instance, should repeat a keyword (such as "Des Moines Pizzeria") often and avoid synonyms (most spiders think "Pizza Shop" and "Pizzeria" are as similar as apples and oranges).

Web sites must also be rich in content (i.e., text). Spiders are designed to prioritize based on depth of information, and they look for sites of authority. This preference is consistent with creating keywords, but it can be confusing. The idea here is to provide an abundance of relevant information about one thing. To a spider, less is not more. For a Web site, it is OK to be wordy as long as you are consistent; just don't be random.

Off the Evolutionary Cliff

Even though we do our best to be the fittest of the fit, nature sometimes throws us a sucker punch. In real life it could come when a dinosaur's DNA urges it to grow bigger than the environment can support, or when the Romans decide to drink wine out of lead cups.

On the Internet, unintentional disasters can happen just as easily. Consider what happened recently to a public company called Answers.com. This Internet bellwether thought it had it made: the company had pretty well figured out what Google wanted and was able to satisfy Google's spiders and algorithms. With that confidence, Answers.com went to great lengths to build as many links to its sites as it could and do so by any means necessary.

But after a while, the wizards at Google began to fine-tune their algorithms to improve the quality of the searches. As I have discussed, the algorithms started looking for things like relevance, longevity, depth of content, and other subjective measures that truly determine relevance. Google started ranking not only the sites but also the links on the sites. It began discounting and even discarding what it considered to be poor links. Minutes after the changes were made, millions of sites were reclassified. The team at Answers.com thought it had all the answers. It worked around the clock to make the appropriate changes to its Web site after Google made its move.

What happened? In July 2007, Answers.com was still a hot Internet company. Its stock was flying high, and it was on the verge of a major acquisition of one of its closest competitors, Dictionary.com, for $100 million.[8] The combined company would have more than 22 million unique visitors each month and would be the twenty-eighth most visited site on the Internet—larger than Craigslist, NBC, CitySearch, Gannett, ESPN, and Cox Communications. It would rank second only to Wikipedia for reference sites.[9]

But all that changed on August 2, when Google changed its search algorithm. Within minutes, Answers.com lost 28 percent of its traffic. On July 2, exactly one month earlier, the stock was at $12. When it announced the search problem, Answers.com stock dropped nearly 50 percent, to $7.76. It continued to fall thereafter, hitting a low of $5.58 a few months later. The company never did close the deal with Dictionary.com, which had been announced only a few short months before.[10]

This happened to no small degree because Answers.com did not understand the Internet as well as it thought—and certainly it didn't understand the brain. It built its castle on the confidence that it could "trick" Google's algorithms. And for a while, it did. But Answers.com failed to realize that the Internet brain is still evolving and that more-complex algorithms would sweep away nutrient-poor Web sites, just as the brain has over the course of evolution.

But the secret to Web sites is not found at Google, nor in a manual on HTML or the Internet; rather, it is found in the brain.

Yes, the World Wide Web is a dangerous place for memes—filled with spiders, viruses, and new, robust Web sites poised to eat their lunch. The worst part is that all this is happening so fast that what worked yesterday, or even this morning, might not work this afternoon.

If you think that situation is bad, I have more bad news for you: it's only going to get worse. For the present, computers are processing information in a serial manner. But when parallel processing becomes the operation *du jour* for most computers, and when Web sites, spiders, viral memes, and all the rest get the kind of network-of-networks intelligence being pioneered by my mentor Jim Anderson, the whole thing will speed up again.

"Memes now spread around the world at the speed of light, and replicate at rates that make even fruit flies and yeast cells look glacial in comparison," Dan Dennett wrote several years ago. "They leap promiscuously from medium to medium, and are proving virtually unquarantinable."[11] That was in 1990—before parallel processing and even before the greatest expansion of the World Wide Web. In the next iteration, memes will be here and there in a blink, flashing off and on faster than fruit flies and yeast cells come and go. One wonders how we will be able to determine good from bad, valuable from destructive—or even find the desired meme in a sea of 100 billion. But a solution is already unfolding, as you will see in the pages that follow.

CHAPTER 7

Searching for the
Right Words

I FIRST MET LARRY PAGE, cofounder of Google, in the lounge at the Fairmont Copley Plaza Hotel in Boston. It was a rainy April day in 2000, and we were attending a conference on the future of search engines.[1] A few years earlier, Page and his cofounder, Sergey Brin, had created a search engine called BackRub, which searched information by analyzing the links that led back to a Web site. The two men were working on it on a shoestring budget, out of—wouldn't you know it—a garage in Silicon Valley.

Most of the conference participants thought that the way to retrieve information from the Internet had to be similar to the way librarians retrieved books from a bin. In fact, Yahoo!, one of the main presenters, had hired droves of librarians to help categorize the entire Internet. Another participant, AltaVista, was building an Internet library that was searchable by keywords. Neither Page nor I had been asked to present at the conference—and so we sat there, in the lounge at the Fairmont, making small talk.[2] (I remember Page suggesting that we work together, and considering the market cap of Google, I regret not falling to my knees immediately and saying yes.)

But had the two of us been asked to speak at the conference, I think we might have added something to the debate.[3] Page, in particular, had a background that could have changed the direction of the talks. When he was working on his PhD at Stanford, his adviser had been Terry Winograd—well known not only as a professor of computer science at Stanford but also as a leading expert in cognitive science. Winograd's books—including *Understanding Natural Language, Language as a Cognitive Process,* and *Understanding Computers and Cognition*—explored the possible bridges between human and computer communication.[4] Page, in other words, was well versed in the brain by the time he founded Google. And if Page needed further explanation of the bond between cognition, language, and computers, he needed look no further than his own father, Carl Victor Page, who was a professor at Michigan State University and an expert in artificial intelligence.

Although we were only vaguely aware of it at the time, Page and I were working along similar lines to find a better way to search the Web. In both cases, our work was driven by the idea that the Internet was evolving as a brain. In Page's case, he realized that the problem with search was not in the categorization of the Internet but in the ranking of the relevance of Web pages.

At the time, this was a revolutionary thought. Most of the search engines were competing to be the one with the largest index of the Web. But does anyone care whether a search engine has categorized the umpteen-millionth Web site? This problem with search, it turns out, is also the biggest problem with the human mind. With all the information the brain stores, how does it make sense of it all?

Google's approach to content, which is largely followed by every major search engine, was to deploy intelligent software to "read" a Web site. Early search engines organized this content by keywords, which can be used to search on a massive scale. While Page and Brin were still at Stanford, Google was already crawling almost fifty pages per second and was able to index sites even faster than that. But the big innovation happened next: the idea that the importance of a Web site is based on how many other Web sites link to it. And it is a matter not only of the *number* of links but also the *quality* of those links, the thinking being that the best Web sites should have many other Web sites that link to them.

Over time, Google's algorithms have evolved and become more powerful. Google now looks at the relevance of a given link and weights the links based on whether they are similar to the Web site's category. A link from SportsIllustrated.com, for instance, is more valuable to a site like Yankees.com than to Amazon.com. Google also looks at the quality of the Web site, such that a link from the Brown Medical School is considered more valuable than Sonny's Backyard Biomedical. This means that the site needs to have links to it by other relevant, high-quality sites. No longer is it good enough for a book or movie to be popular; now it must be critically acclaimed, with a starred review or two thumbs up.

Does that sound familiar? It should, because that is how the brain works: the *best* neurons, those with the richest connections, have the most links to other neurons around them. That's also the essence of the selfish meme theory of Richard Dawkins.

It underscores another thought: in order for the Internet to be a brain, it had to learn to communicate, just as humans did thousands of years ago. Words, after all, are the fundamental unit of human intelligence, and language is the foundation of civilization. Sigmund Freud had it right when he said, "The first human who hurled an insult instead of a stone was the founder of civilization."

Speaking in words is a uniquely human accomplishment, something that no other animal, nor even a computer, has mastered. But on the Internet, and through the work of Google and other Internet whizzes, language is turning the Internet into a civilized brain. Understanding how Google reads Web sites is the best way to understand the Internet and leverage it to your advantage.

Calling Henry Higgins

How did Google learn to use words to communicate with Web sites? It's an incredibly difficult task. Google must read a Web page, interpret its meaning, and then determine its relevance to a keyword that users have entered. How do you do that? Well, since my first company, Simpli.com, helped invent some of the technology to make this possible, I'll explain how we did it.[5]

The ideas all converged on a winter day in 1999. That afternoon, a man nearing his nineties shuffled into our offices at Brown University. At the time, my team was trying to build a search engine that would do a better job of finding information on the Web. Every quest needs a wizard, and that day I met mine. His name was

George Miller. He had come from Princeton, where he was a professor of linguistics (and won the National Medal of Science).[6]

Miller, a linguist, had developed an innovative piece of software called WordNet, a bold attempt to categorize and store human language in computers in a way similar to the way the brain stores language.[7] If search engines could use this technology, then they would be able to interpret the meaning of a search. This was exactly the problem that people were having with the Internet before Google. Searchers had to jump from one search engine to another, and none of them was very satisfying. But suppose my group could do better? Suppose we could help the Internet communicate with our brains?

You may wonder what a linguist has to do with the Internet. Perhaps you have never met a linguist in real life and assume linguists must be something on the order of *My Fair Lady*'s Professor Henry Higgins, a reedy character in a herringbone suit with the nasty habit of correcting your elocution (what?) in public. You wouldn't want to sit next to one at a dinner party. But at the risk of overstating the case, linguists have become the Indiana Joneses of brain science—explorers of the unknown.

Why? It's because words are the most direct communication we have from the mind. They are symbols of thought that are blown from one of us to the other, like smoke signals emerging from the mouth of a dark cave. In our everyday lives, we take words and sentences for granted. As Chinese emperor Chuang-Tzu once said, "The rabbit snare exists because of the rabbit; once you've gotten the rabbit, you can forget the snare. Words exist because of meaning; once you've gotten the meaning you can forget the words."

For linguists, the study of language, grammar, and the logic and reason implicit within them holds secrets to the workings of the mind. They teach us not only how we choose to describe the world but also how we retrieve information and how we structure words into sentences and sentences into paragraphs. It reveals the logic behind thought—and, of course, the illogic that makes human beings human.

We cannot have an intelligent Internet that cannot understand language. But understanding language is not as easy as merely learning words. As Harvard psychologist Steven Pinker notes, "If there is a bag in your car, and a gallon of milk in the bag, there is a gallon of milk in your car. But if there's a person in your car, and a gallon of blood in a person, it would be strange to conclude that there is a gallon of blood in your car."[8]

Or consider this joke: "Two friends are sitting at a bar drinking, and one turns to the other and says, 'Joe, I think you've had enough—your face is turning blurry.'"[9] It might take the hundred billion neurons residing in your cerebral cortex a second or two to get it. But the chances are good that no computer, regardless of its vaunted silicon IQ, would understand. Those are the kinds of language and thinking clues that a thinking machine would need to pick up on. Otherwise, for all of its billions of circuits—gulping electricity and making calculations a million times as fast as the neurons in a brain—it is still a silly fool.

And that is exactly what Miller and my team were working on as we tried to "teach" search engines like Google to read and understand Web pages. The idea stemmed from an expanded version of WordNet. WordNet represented knowledge and words in a series of hierarchies that helped link together the context of words. Consider the following:

vehicle > motor vehicle > automobile = auto = car > sports car > Porsche > 911, 944, Boxster

Almost every word in natural language has both generalizations and specializations of this kind. These relationships form a network structure. The power of a network representation is that it puts specific information in a more general framework that can be used to compute answers to queries. In a typical search engine, if a user types *Boxster*, the only term that can be searched is *Boxster*. But if we use the network structure of WordNet, we can also activate the *sports car* and *Porsche* nodes (which elicit even more robust information) and quickly discover that Boxsters have high-powered engines, usually seat two people, and aren't exactly cheap.

Of course, there is an more serious problem with language, namely that words are ambiguous. If words used in natural language had single, well-defined meanings, life would be simpler. Unfortunately, that is not the case. Language is a complex, ever-evolving instrument, and a quick look at a dictionary will show that essentially all common words have multiple meanings. In fact, the more frequently a word is used, the more meanings it is likely to have. (Linguists call the occurrence of multiple meanings for a word *polysemy*, not to be confused with a similar-sounding word for having multiple wives.) It is a truism in linguistics that each word means something slightly different. As we have learned with memes and Web sites, if two words have exactly the same meaning, one will vanish, as can be observed historically.

Consider the two words *board* and *plank*. Both can refer to pieces of wood. The two statements, "He went to The Home Depot and purchased a knotty pine *board*" and "He went to The Home Depot and purchased a knotty pine *plank*" mean about the same thing. However, both *board* and *plank* have multiple meanings, and these other meanings are completely different. For example, *board* and *plank* are not synonyms in the following sentence: "The venture capitalist will throw the CEO off a *plank* if he is not elected to the *board* of the corporation."

We humans deal with this situation very well. For example, if we are speakers of English, when we hear the three words *bat, ball*, and *diamond* we know that the topic is almost surely related to baseball, even though all the words in the string are ambiguous. *Bat* could refer to flying mammals, *diamond* to a gem or a shape, and *ball* to a party or a sphere. The common association of the words in the string—baseball—can be determined immediately by a knowledgeable observer using both the context formed by the group of words and the observer's knowledge about the world.

Unconscious contextual disambiguation—choosing the right meaning of words having many possible meanings—is something people do effortlessly. However, this problem is so difficult for computers that it stopped early attempts at artificial intelligence dead in its tracks. A word is surrounded by an invisible cloud of context, along with world knowledge that can be used by a human but is not available to a computer.

WordNet deals with multiple word meanings by the formation of what are called *synsets*—that is, sets of synonyms. Each synset consists of groups of words that share a particular meaning; they act as synonyms, but only for a single meaning. To follow up on our example, *board* and *plank* form a synset when referring to the meaning "pieces of wood." However, both *board* and *plank* have other meanings that are not shared—for example, *board* as in "board of directors," and *plank* as in "part of a pirate ship."

We used WordNet to solve the problem of search through a process called spreading activation.[10] *Spreading activation* is a process by which closely connected words "wire and fire together." The basic architecture allows effective use of this computational technique in the worlds of cognitive science and neural networks. Spreading activation assumes that some kind of "excitation" spreads from node to node in the network via the links between nodes. The spread is limited to a local area using various techniques so that when someone says *bat* and *baseball*, only the other related terms get activated (*diamond* and not *flying mammal*). (From a technical standpoint, spreading activation is mathematically powerful and also allows contact with a useful body of neural network theory. This contact allows links as well as nodes to have weights, that is, continuous values.)

Recall from chapter 6 the importance of semantic networks. These networks are essentially maps that our brains use to navigate information in our minds. WordNet approximates these maps by using synsets that allow the Internet to build context into language through spreading activation. As one example of how spreading activation might be useful, consider the "bat, ball, diamond" example. Each word has multiple meanings. Yet each word contains a meaning linked to baseball among its sets of meanings. If we simply excite links connected to each meaning, the *baseball* node will get three times as much excitation as the meanings that are not common to all the words.[11]

For a more practical e-commerce example, consider someone who is searching for shirts, pants, and jackets. All these items have *clothing* as a superordinate category. If each of these specific terms spreads activation to parts of the network connected to it, *clothing* will be activated three times, once from each subordinate. For e-commerce, such a computation is valuable because we know that shirts are rarely sold in "shirt stores" or pants in "pants stores," but both are found in clothing stores. Knowing the right level of generality—that is, the store type—to look for (in either e-commerce or regular commerce) is a matter of great importance, and computers often have difficulty determining the right level without help.

Without this intelligence, search engines are bound to make all kinds of mistakes. It brings to mind the first version of Google's advertising system, which inadvertently placed a luggage ad on a news article describing how a woman was murdered and stuffed into a suitcase.[12] Virtually all search engines now use some of these techniques to make their engines and algorithms "smart."

Zipf's Law and the Long Tail

To create a proxy for popularity, Google and other search engines now tie word meanings to frequency of use. This technique enables the search engine to order and rank results. Word frequency, word usage, and word meaning frequency are related statistically by an experimentally observed relationship called Zipf's law.[13] Zipf's law predicts that more-frequent words are used a great deal more often than less-frequent words. When word rank (most frequent word, second most frequent word, etc.) is plotted against the frequency of occurrence of the word, the resulting curve is roughly a hyperbola. This relationship means that the hundredth most common word occurs at roughly one-hundredth of the frequency of the most common word. This is a very rapid drop in frequency of occurrence. Despite its importance, it is not known why Zipf's law relations occur so often in language.

A Zipf's law relationship also holds for the degree of ambiguity of words. The more frequently a word appears in text, the more different meanings it has. This leads to the curious paradox that the most common words are also the most ambiguous. As a result, trying to write clear speech using simple, common words is considerably more difficult than it first appears. In contrast, precise technical terms occur with very low frequency but also tend to be unambiguous. This is one of the reasons academics have an easy time writing scientific journal articles that very few people understand and find it difficult to write a general-interest book that is easy to read.

Zipf's law is directly relevant to Internet searches, because the number of accesses of a particular Web page also follows Zipf's law. That is, the most common pages are accessed very frequently, and the bulk of Web pages are almost never seen. The top ten thousand most frequently accessed Web pages constitute a significant fraction of total page views. It is this statistical property that lets search engines like Yahoo!, Ask Jeeves, and Mahalo "hand code" particularly important Web pages and not lose as much retrieval power as might be expected.

There has been a lot of talk about how the Internet has driven a concept called "the long tail," an idea based on a book by Chris Anderson suggesting that less-popular information and goods are becoming more relevant because of the Internet.[14] And there is strong evidence to support this notion. Just look at the variety of music available on iTunes or the sheer quantity of random, formerly out of print books at Amazon.com. But the long tail does not apply generally to the Internet, Web sites, or search. There is still a strong bell curve there, driven by Zipf's law.

Natural Selection

The Internet is a competitive place, a jungle where various Web sites vie for dominance and survival. Just as in nature—where plants have developed luscious fruits, fragrances, and advantages to lure beneficial life forms to them (as well as thorns and poisons to repel harmful life forms)—so have the competing sites on the Internet resorted to subterfuge to better their chances of replication and survival.

As they enter this jungle, search engines are looking for meaning in Web sites and so, too, must the Web sites have meaning. What, for instance, could be more nutrient poor for a Web site than to be a credit card solicitation from a bank? Search engine spiders are relentless in identifying such Web sites—sites that will not only sicken the recipient of that meme (who doesn't want it) but also will eventually kill the search engine (because consumers will move to another search engine). So search engines, especially clever ones like Google, are made to find things like credit card solicitations and spit them out.

But the credit card companies are themselves ruthlessly trying to survive. Last year, Americans received six billion credit card offers through direct mail, each one cleverly tailored to the tastes and demographics of the recipient.[15] Yet just as the credit card companies have mastered their form of mass invasion, the response from direct mail is falling off. More Americans, it seems, are turning to the Internet to make their purchases.

At first, the credit card companies jumped blindly into Internet marketing using the same techniques of pushing credit cards on to consumers. But then they began to see their folly: in terms of the natural selection of a meme, a credit card solicitation is an evolutionary disaster, a meme that is not wanted. In the evolutionary sense, it is an apple seed without an apple; pollen on the stamen, without the fragrance to attract the bee.

To make their sites more attractive, card companies have become adept at adding content that will make them more nutritious. HSBC bank, for instance, has a Web site called Your Point of View.com, which offers visitors information on topics such as global warming (including blog sites where visitors can log in their opinions). They can click on "The Climate Partnership," a link that explores HSBC's support of several environmental groups.

Users can even participate in polls on such provocative questions as, "Are we too busy to have kids?" or "Would you go into business with your family?" All this, like the fruit of an apple, is designed to lure consumers to bite in and, in doing so, spread the seed. HBSC is not alone. American Express has its Discovery site, which offers a Google-like search engine; Chase offers students reward points when they apply for a card online, and additional points when they convince a friend to apply. Chase has even created a "shopping engine" on Facebook where card applicants can exchange points for various products.

That's not all. Some marketers have learned about Google's linking algorithms and have created fake Web sites that link to other Web sites to artificially increase the rankings of their pages. These are not your traditional marketers who graduated with an MBA from Northwestern, spent ten years at Procter & Gamble, and are now trying to leverage the Internet. These marketers are "technologists gone bad."

A few years ago, I met a sixteen-year-old computer whiz making $3 million a year from his parents' house. I asked him what he sold, and he said, "Nothing." What he was doing was exploiting a loophole in Google that allows people to create affiliate sites that act as proxies for other people's products. If you search for contractors on Google, four of the first five results are all affiliates (one of them is a partnership with famed TV home improvement maven Bob Vila, run by one of my companies). They sell nothing but instead redirect people to others offering goods and services. This crafty young marketeer built thousands of affiliate sites, linked them to one another, and then paid others to link to his sites. Once he started getting free traffic from Google, he sold that traffic to the *real* marketers at Procter & Gamble, American Express, Chase, and HSBC.

This trick, although clever, destroys the value of Google's algorithms, just as a bad idea or schizophrenia can corrupt the mind. As a result, Google has started to evolve into a more intelligent memory retrieval system. It tries to weed out these spoof sites by looking at the content on Web pages. Google checks how many times content is updated, how similar the content is, and which sites it links to. It is now easy for a company to pay a third party for links, partner with someone to share links, or simply create what are sarcastically called "link farms": Web sites with nothing but a large number of random links. All these techniques work well to deceive Google and the search engines. But this is a game of cat and mouse.

Just as we have a tangle of competitive interests in the outside world, so do we have it in the mind. The human brain constantly weighs information in a mental battle that we are rarely aware of (until it reaches the stage where we literally need a vacation, or perhaps a hot shower, to try to straighten out our thoughts). How many times do we feel bombarded—by the shrill voices on TV, the sound of jets screaming overhead? How often do we need some "quality time" just to set our minds on the good stuff—seeing a friend, reading a good book, contemplating where we are going with our lives?

In their own way, Google's algorithms are mimicking the brain's need to clear out the clutter and find the good stuff. Google's approach to link relevance works precisely the way a simple neural network works. Links between neurons are weighted based on how relevant (or connected) they are to one another, and that weighting triggers or suppresses activity. Google uses a similar structure to rank or suppress Web sites through its search results.

The Attack of the Creepy Crawlies

This kind of intelligent search technology was what the Google founders were building when I first met them in Boston, and it is why we keep coming back to them. It turns out that Web sites, like memory, are only as good as the search mechanisms that enable them to be retrieved. An amnesic has no use for her memory, because she cannot retrieve it (assuming it is still there). And a Web site is irrelevant—as a neuron, a meme, or a vehicle for e-commerce—if it is not retrievable. In the chaos of the Internet (it is fair to say that 800 percent growth and 100 million Web sites count as chaos), order comes in the form of a search and rescue mission. (For that matter, we may as well call the World Wide Web the Wild Wild West. We can keep the WWW.) The great land grab on the Internet was always about search, and virtually every leading company—including AOL, Yahoo!, Microsoft, Amazon.com, and Google—tried to join the footrace.

It turns out that Google has already won the race. Google does more searches every day than all other Internet search engines combined, including Yahoo!, Ask Jeeves, MSN, and any other one you can think of. As the others lost the battle, they joined Google's fray by trying to build Web sites that ranked high in the very search engine that they were competing against. They couldn't beat 'em, so they joined 'em, as countless companies began building their sites around Google's algorithms and partnering with it for advertising. This level of coverage is what has made Google both dominant and frightening (and made its employees rich beyond belief— more than a thousand Google millionaires and counting, including the in-house masseuse).[16]

You may say that Google is a human-made, rational enterprise. But Google also has an evolutionary imperative: there are many search engines, after all, and all of them are competing to deliver the most content-rich material to their consumers. A search engine that rewards users with lots of information will be used again. One whose searches are wrong, inconsistent, or filled with nutrient-poor spam will fail. Natural selection is at work at this level.

So it is no wonder that search engines craft their spiders well: in the ability of the algorithms to discern rich Web site content from poor Web site content lies the ability of the search engine itself to survive. At the top of the algorithmic food chain is Google. Surprisingly, however, even though people perform more searches on Google than on all the other search engines combined, Google searches represent only 2 percent of time spent online. This is because Google does its job very well: users search, find what they are looking for, and leave. Compare that with Yahoo!, which has roughly one-tenth of the search traffic but holds its users hostage for six times as long as does Google.[17]

The Prom Queen

So the best sites filter to the top because they have the best, and arguably most useful, content—right? If it were only that easy, we would all have modestly mediocre sites. But things are far more complex than that. As you have seen, the most important function of Google is to count the number of links to and from your Web site and use them as a proxy for relevance.

The primary innovation from Google in this regard is something it calls PageRank, which ranks pages based on the number of external links to a site. Recall that neurons determine the relevance of information, and the most popular and useful neurons have the greatest number of dendrites. In Google's early attempts, it simply counted the number of links to determine how relevant (or popular) a given site was. This method works in principle because it is used by each of us all the time: we watch movies because they are box office hits and read books because they are best sellers.

It is a strange recursive loop indeed, where neurons get stronger because they are strong, and Web sites are ranked higher because they have a high rank, and books are bought because they have sold well, and movies are watched because everyone has seen them. We have entered a world where the rich always get richer and the popular girl is prom queen. According to the gang at Google, "PageRank relies on . . . the web by using its vast link structure as an indicator of an individual page's value. In essence, Google interprets a link from page A to page B as a vote, by page A, for page B. But, Google looks at more than the sheer volume of votes, or links a page receives; it also analyzes the page that casts the vote. Votes cast by pages that are themselves 'important' weigh more heavily and help to make other pages 'important.'"[18]

This description may not pass muster in a democratic election, but it would make any neuroscientist proud.

CHAPTER 8

The Limits of Networks

Now THAT THAT WE'VE unlocked the possibilities of the Internet, I must throw in a caveat: networks, despite our current excitement over Facebook, Twitter, and even such mainstays as MySpace and YouTube, have an inherent flaw—a ticking time bomb that most investors and many in the industry prefer not to face. Just as the human brain grows rapidly in infancy and then shrinks, so do networks of all kinds, including (and especially) Internet networks. Despite the cheerleading from these companies, they will not grow forever. It's important to remember this if you are building a network, you're an investor, or you are merely hitching your star to someone else's network.

The good news is that networks may not grow forever, but they do follow the curve of the human brain: even when they are getting smaller, they supplant quantity with quality. Yes, just as humans find wisdom in old age, networks do as well.

The lesson in this is that even though all networks stop growing, they grow stronger as they age. To explain this better, let me tell you about Bob Metcalfe, one of the Internet's foremost inventors and pundits.

Metcalfe's Law and the Laws of Gravity

In 1979, MIT grad Bob Metcalfe started a company based on a computer networking standard (called Ethernet) that he had invented while pursuing his PhD. Ethernet not only linked personal computers but also sent packages of data from one machine to another in an efficient network.

But because Ethernet systems weren't cheap—about $5,000 each—Metcalfe was left with a vexing problem: he had to convince his customers that the more money they spent and the more Ethernet connections they bought, the more they would benefit. It was just like fax machines. One fax machine isn't any good. Two are minimal. But it's when you have thousands that the network makes sense. That was Metcalfe's case, and to press the point, he created a graph to illustrate his argument. It loosely stated that "the power of a computer network increases at roughly the square of the number of devices connected to it." The original Metcalfe slide is shown in figure 8-1.

Before long, Ethernet was a huge success, adopted everywhere in the burgeoning personal computer industry. Metcalfe's company, 3Com, went public in 1984 and became largely responsible for the proliferation of the Internet worldwide in the early 1990s.

FIGURE 8-1

The original Metcalfe's law

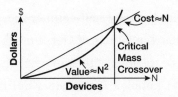

Source: Adapted from Robert M. Metcalfe, "It's all in Your Head," *Forbes*, May 7, 2007.

Clearly, Metcalfe was not your run-of-the-mill visionary, and so people took him very seriously. In 1993, George Gilder, a columnist for *Forbes*, picked up on Metcalfe's hypothesis, changed "devices" to "users," and hailed the equation as "Metcalfe's Law."[1] By 1996, Vice President Al Gore, delivering the commencement address at MIT, changed "users" to "people" and evoked Metcalfe's law to demonstrate the power of the information highway.[2] Before long, "Metcalfe's law" was on everyone's lips.

In essence, Metcalfe's law stated two powerful things: one was that the Internet would grow forever. This assertion fit neatly into the mounting concept that there was a "new economy" afoot, one that didn't obey the laws and limitations of the old economy. Thus, in the case of the Internet, the more people (or users or devices) who hooked on, the bigger the thing would get.

Second, Metcalfe's law said that the *first movers*—the companies that first got people hooked up to networks—would rule the roost. The theory was similar to that argued in 1908 by Theodore Vail, then president of Bell Telephone, when he stated that the more telephone users under the Bell logo, the better for Bell and for the country, and for that the company received a monopoly on telephone services. In 1917 a Bell employee named Lytkins nailed this down in a paper on the "economics of network effects," and that's where it sat for the next half-century or so.[3]

But by the 1990s, the effects of Metcalfe's law were far greater. It not only supported the idea of the new economy but also pumped air into the Internet bubble.[4] If the important thing was to be the first to establish the network, then what was important in business? The key was being a first mover. Hence companies rushed into new markets, and investors shoveled billions of dollars into new ideas.

What about profits? Who cares, management said smugly. What counted was the first mover advantage—to have the biggest market share, at whatever the cost, profits be damned. But then the laws of gravity trumped Metcalfe's law, and the bubble burst. Billions in market cap were washed away. Metcalf, true to form, was unrepentant. "Al Gore and I may not have invented the Internet," he said a few years ago with a chuckle, "but we invented the Internet Bubble."[5]

Metcalfe's Revenge

That might have been the end of the story. But now the Internet is alive again, and, if it isn't Webvan or Pets.com that are the Internet darlings, it is Facebook and the other social networks. This time around, the layout of the Internet is different. Back then it was driven by individual Web sites, such as the venerable Amazon.com, eBay, and Yahoo! But with the era of social networks has come the era of *networks of networks*. These are Web sites, maintained by individuals, that link into other Web sites. Like my

FIGURE 8-2

The people in a social network

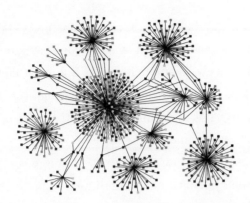

Source: Adapted from http://prblog.typepad.com/strategic_public_relation/images/2007/06/22/simple_ social_network.png.

mentor Jim Anderson's original neural network model, social networks break the Web into subgroups of participating people and Web sites. But in the case of social networks, entrepreneurs swapped neurons and memes for people. Those people, connected in social networks, resemble something like figure 8-2.

Now that Metcalfe's law is on the loose again, is it valid? Will it raise irrational exuberance for social networking to the fever pitch of the Internet bubble, and will it have the same dire consequences?

The Law of Equilibrium

My take is that Metcalfe's law, while not wrong, is incomplete. Metcalfe's law speaks only to the early stage of a network's growth, when bigger is always better, often exponentially so.[6] The law currently holds in situations like computing and the Internet, but it breaks down with established networks, and it will eventually break down on the Internet as the Internet becomes more established.

The truth is that bigger networks are not always better. During the growth phase, networks become (roughly) exponentially more valuable as they grow. That much is true. But eventually they reach a state of critical mass and then seek equilibrium (or they implode and companies go out of business). It is at the point of equilibrium that a network is at its most powerful.

To explain this, I defer again to the brain: when we are conceived, the brain begins a nine-month race to produce neurons, a pace that equals about 250,000 neurons per minute.[7] If the rest of our body's cells grew at an equal rate, it is said, we would be ten feet tall and weigh some 250 pounds at birth (sorry Mom).

The brain continues to grow after birth, but after the first three months something extraordinary occurs: the brain reaches the edge of the envelope. Its rate of growth slows. Why? For one thing, the skull isn't big enough to accommodate a brain that continued to grow exponentially. Perhaps nature realized that if we couldn't hold up our heads well enough to run, the additional smarts weren't going to get us very far. In any case, the brain, which weighs around three hundred grams at birth (10 percent of our body weight), reaches its full weight of fourteen hundred grams (less than 2 percent of our body weight) by the time we are teenagers.[8]

Then something even stranger happens. Just as we enter our twenties, when we would expect the brain to really kick in, it balances out—a process of seeking the optimal state of equilibrium. By the time we are twenty, the growth of the brain actually reverses. From that time until the end of our lives, we lose about one gram of brain weight every year.[9] And we wind up with some 100 trillion neural connections, compared with the 10 quadrillion of a three-year-old.[10]

So are adults smarter than three-year-olds? Thankfully, yes, because the remaining connections between the neurons grow stronger and patterns of neurons are formed, and from all this comes . . . wisdom. Let the kids have the quadrillions of neurons that enable "fast and frugal" learning; adults have the evolutionary elegance of the mature brain.

If we apply Metcalfe's law to the brain, we see that it applies to neurons until birth (the connections between the neurons continue growing exponentially until the age of about three). After that, a different law applies to the brain—that of equilibrium. In the brain, this means a period of slowing growth and eventually a process of decline.

But when the brain has stopped growing and reaches a point of equilibrium, it gains intelligence. At the ripe old age of three, for instance, my son shocks me with how much he knows. But that's because he has no filters. He remembers all kinds of things. Soon, he will start asking "why" about everything. But this phase (thankfully) won't last. His neural development will actually slow. By the time he becomes an intelligent (yet unpredictable) teenager, he will have stopped asking why—and will start thinking more for himself.

What's interesting is that this process can be seen in other networks, as diverse as bees, termites, and ants. Ants, for example, form large colonies that become, no surprise, exponentially stronger the larger they grow. The bigger colonies do better at foraging for food, protecting the queen, and communicating. Some colonies grow to have as many as a million ants.[11]

Yes, Metcalfe's law applies to ants . . . to a point. Once these colonies reach critical mass, they stop growing. Critical mass is determined by a number of factors, such as how much food is available, how much terrain needs to be foraged, and how many competing colonies are nearby. As these factors change, the colonies evolve. What you then see is an ebb and flow of new members joining and dying, creating a natural state of equilibrium. This cycle is true not only of ants but also of termites, bees, wasps, and virtually all social animals.[12]

It turns out that the same rules apply for human-made constructs. Anyone who drives in cities such as London, Los Angeles, or Atlanta must wonder why traffic is so bad. The answer is that highways are networks, and this means that bigger is not always better. The old wives' tale of "just add another lane" doesn't really work. Here is how one journalist put it, referring to a recently published article in *Nature*: "A recent paper establish[es] an interesting paradox about the flow of vehicular traffic: adding a new road segment to an existing network of roadways can under certain circumstances reduce the car-carrying capacity of the network as a whole . . . It turns out that the properties collectively exhibited by large numbers of cars moving over a network of roadways have many mathematical features in common with the behavior of other things that flow over networks, such as data carried by telephone lines and the Internet."[13]

In the landmark book *Emergence*, Steven Johnson argues that the modern city is suspiciously similar to the brain in its network behavior.[14] Many of Johnson's insights came from urban planning critic Jane Jacobs, who urged city planners during the 1960s to build dense urban cores, noting that as they did so, cities would grow stronger.[15] That was Metcalfe's law, circa the 1960s. *New*

Yorker columnist Lewis Mumford reminded Jacobs, however, that if they grow too dense, cities can reach a point of diminishing returns: "Jacobs forgets that in organisms there is no tissue growth quite as 'vital' or 'dynamic' as cancer growths . . . The author has forgotten the most essential characteristic of all organic growth— to maintain diversity and balance, the organism must not exceed the norm of its species. Any ecological association eventually reaches the 'climax stage,' beyond which growth without deterioration is not possible."[16]

In other words, this principle exists in all networks: cities, highways, ants, bees, and the brain alike.

The Laws of Networking

What does this mean for the Internet? My theory is that Metcalfe's law works until a network reaches the point of critical mass. But at that point—where cost exceeds value—the value curve stops increasing. The value curve almost inevitably follows the cost curve from that point forward.[17] (As an aside, the cost curve is no longer considered to be linear, because there are significant economies of scale involved with larger networks, so following the cost curve does not necessarily imply a linear incline.) Once that inflection point is reached, the network must achieve equilibrium or else it will implode. In some cases, such as ants and cities, equilibrium regulates the system to a point of critical mass; in others, such as the brain, growth is followed by a period of decline.

Thus, networks essentially have three stages. In each one, different rules apply.

1. **The big bang:** The Internet, ant colonies, and the brain all have periods of rapid expansion. Let's call this the big bang

period. During this period, Metcalfe's law holds true. It is best during this time to allow the network to grow unencumbered. Pruning the network or stunting its growth is dangerous at this time, because you do not know what should be pruned. The brain does not do that, and neither should any other network for fear of chopping off the wrong limb.

2. **The collapse:** Because it is not possible to prune a network during its growth phase, eventually a network will grow to be too large. At this point, one of two things will happen. Either it will implode (over time, the brain loses half its neurons and well over half its connections), or its growth will slow rapidly (as with ant colonies).[18] As you see the network slowing, let it slow. You can even begin pruning the weakest links and nodes (the brain naturally does this using something called *cellular suicide*). Whatever the network, as it enters this stage, you should allow it to stabilize instead of pushing for further growth.

3. **The equilibrium:** In this stage, networks reach a point of equilibrium, where they oscillate roughly around a certain size. It is during this stage that networks are at their peak performance. This does not mean that a network will suffer the fate of a slowing company, because when a network slows, other things—such as communication, intelligence, and consciousness—gain speed. For the brain, this happens at roughly 100 billion neurons and 100 trillion connections. For the Internet and its Web sites, who knows? But it will eventually happen.

Why should anyone believe that the Internet will move through its big bang and possibly even collapse? It hasn't happened yet, and Metcalfe's law predicts that it won't happen. And what does it matter anyway? How will someone building a Web site or company on the Internet benefit by knowing that it will eventually destruct?

I can't show you proof of something that has not yet happened. But in chapter 9, I will show you examples of networks that follow this pattern over and over on the Internet. This process is a natural phenomenon: a part of evolution itself, replicated in the biology of the brain. So when it happens in artificial environments, such as the Web, it is best to stand out of the way and embrace it.

CHAPTER 9

The Social Networks

I HAVE A LOT in common with Richard Rosenblatt. We are about the same age, are both entrepreneurs, and have both run public and private companies. We also share the kind of eternal optimism that irks many people. But what sets Rosenblatt apart from me is that he was chairman of MySpace, one of the most widely publicized companies in the world of social networking.

Rosenblatt cut his teeth with DrKoop.com and iMALL, the second of which was sold very profitably to Excite.[1] After that he managed eUniverse, a company that once had looked forward to a bright future until it was mismanaged and delisted from the NASDAQ exchange. That was when Rosenblatt jumped in.[2]

Rosenblatt doesn't look for problems within companies; he looks for opportunities. So when he took over at eUniverse, he changed the name to Intermix, got it back on the NASDAQ, and looked for assets in the company that he could exploit. One of those was a little-known site called MySpace.

MySpace was created by two employees at Intermix after they saw the huge success of Friendster and Classmates.com.[3] Under Rosenblatt's leadership, MySpace grew to more than two million members within a few months.[4] But for all its success, MySpace was still third in size behind Classmates.com and Friendster.

Long Live MySpace

How did MySpace beat Classmates.com and Friendster and come to dominate the world of social networking? Because I worked at United Online when we bought Classmates, let me start there and tell you how it happened from my perspective.

Classmates.com was founded by Randy Conrads in 1995 to serve, you guessed it, former high school classmates trying to reunite. The site was free to use and had great success in driving traffic. But like many Internet companies, it had very little advertising revenue to support the business. Then the founders changed the business model and started charging for access to certain parts of the network. That made Classmates.com profitable by 2001, but made it vulnerable to free social networks.

By the time United Online took over Classmates.com in 2001, it had 1.4 million paying subscribers and nearly 38 million registered users. It was here that the team made the decision to focus on profits at the expense of the first stage of networks, Metcalfe's big bang—namely, that one should grow a network unencumbered.

By focusing on profits instead of the growth of the network, United let Friendster and MySpace eclipse Classmates in size, although it became and still is to this day one of the only profitable networks.[5]

As for Friendster, MySpace beat that site for a different reason. Founded in 2002 by Jonathan Abrams, Friendster was the dominant social network by 2003. Although Classmates.com was largely considered the first social network, many people credited Friendster with the launch of Web 2.0 and hailed Abrams as an Internet wunderkind. *Time* flagged Friendster as one of the best inventions of 2003, and *Entertainment Weekly* hailed Abrams as "the friendliest man of the year."[6]

In fact, Friendster was enjoying a meteoric rise in both media attention and growth. The company tapped no less than Tim Koogle, former CEO of Yahoo!, to take the reins as CEO. As with most growing networks, the growth was akin to a brain's neural development in the early stages—fast and furious. Here was a company poised for success.

But the growth was so large and so fast that it nearly brought the company's technology to a halt. Load times, for instance, typically exceeded a minute per page.[7] But that is not what killed Friendster, nor, as many people assume, was the great success of MySpace the reason for its demise.

In addition to technical problems Friendster was hit by a phenomenon called *fakesters*. These were fake profiles set up by charlatans. One hacker pretended to be Bill Gates; another, Bill Clinton. Others included Jesus, Elvis, and R2D2. Although these fakesters were phonies, their sites were wildly popular.[8] But Abrams, the young and somewhat abrasive founder, wanted the fakesters " . . . all gone. All of them."[9]

But removing the fakesters cut off thousands of connections within the network, leaving abandoned many other legitimate profiles that were linked to them. If Abrams had been more familiar with neuroscience, he might have realized that Friendster was killing its most popular neurons. But he didn't—and that's when the founders at MySpace jumped in.

Recognizing that Friendster was going down the wrong path, MySpace embraced the fakesters.[10] As far as it was concerned, users could befriend their neighbors, Barack Obama, or even Ronald McDonald. Within months of this decision, MySpace's users surpassed Friendster's, and within a year, MySpace had twenty-two million users to Friendster's one million.[11] These days, MySpace has more than one hundred million users (meager only if compared to the U.S. population of three hundred million).[12] MySpace sees more traffic than Google and signs up more users every day than the populations of Green Bay and Kansas City combined.[13]

Will MySpace Implode?

By following the laws of networking, MySpace became a phenomenon and eventually was sold to Rupert Murdoch's News Corp in July 2005 for nearly $600 million.[14] Less than a year later, Google cut an ad deal with MySpace worth a reported $900 million.[15] In 2006, Murdoch said that MySpace was worth more than $6 billion.[16] And MySpace continues to grow, following the curve of Metcalfe's law.

Now, however, you can see signs that MySpace is exceeding the inflection point of networks. Not including the highly publicized child pornography problem, security issues are growing graver, highlighted in 2008 when more than a half million user pictures were uploaded to another site.[17] Because anyone can build and create a page on MySpace, consistency is lacking and searching is growing more difficult. And even though MySpace continues to grow, by early 2008 MySpace had begun to see a slowdown in the rate of its user growth.[18]

But the core problem, ironically, is that MySpace continues to grow at all. MySpace is likely past the inflection point for a network. This is causing all sorts of user problems that should result in constriction, but the MySpace team is fighting it. My sense is that it should stop growing now—before it implodes. To be sure, MySpace is in a heated battle with a new competitor, and on the Internet, for better or worse, the perception is that size matters.

So MySpace is pushing to increase usage, traffic, and registered users. But this practice is causing problems that will frustrate users and ultimately destroy the network. The biggest problem is that the network is becoming untenable and unnatural. When you join a social network such as MySpace, you expect to connect with people you know, reconnect with those you have known, and reach out to those you want to know. The community grows and thrives based on those three assumptions. But when a network grows too large, your ability to connect to others becomes overwhelming. If you search for John Smith on MySpace, you will receive five hundred pages of names (roughly five thousand people), but only because MySpace caps the number of pages per search at five hundred. Hopefully you are not John the 5001st, and heaven forbid if you are trying to find someone named John Smith.[19]

Users are constantly bombarded with requests to befriend people they do not know. Occasionally, this is not a bad thing. Who isn't touched by having someone reach out to be friends? But imagine getting such solicitations numerous times per month, per week, per day, and even per hour. The value of a network does not increase with size when the size of the network makes it impossible to derive value from it.

Even worse, because of the numbers of people trolling on MySpace (and the lack of restrictions), it is easy for someone to find you randomly. Predators, in particular, are on the site looking for money, credit, computer fraud, or sex. The nation saw the horrifying effects of this when *Dateline NBC* aired a recurring segment on child pornography called "To Catch a Predator," which showed child molesters using MySpace and other sites to meet unsuspecting children. The danger has become so serious on MySpace that forty-nine U.S. attorneys general banded together in 2008 to issue guidelines for social networking.[20]

I suspect that what is happening on MySpace is the following (I say "suspect" because independent sources of user data are notoriously unreliable). The number of registered users continues to grow, but the number of active users is likely stalling. This is because curiosity continues to prompt new users to try the network, but many find it too overwhelming to be useful. These new users, along with large groups of existing users who have seen a decrease in value because of the new users, will likely become inactive.

As a former MySpace user, I can attest to a decreasing value because of the size of the network. Certainly, heavy users and those who have established strong relationships on MySpace will continue to be very active, but they will not necessarily gain value from the increased size of the network—a sure sign that Metcalfe's law is no longer relevant.

MySpace execs are likely struggling with a network that has reached its equilibrium point. They should be weeding out the low-impact, inactive, and irrelevant users, just as the brain weeds out the least-viable neurons through a process aptly called cellular suicide. Now is the time for pruning.

MySpace should also be limiting users' ability to connect with others in an effort to match the growth of the network to the value curve. This approach is different from artificially cutting the network because of an ideological concern (such as what happened to Friendster); this is genetic fitness, à la cellular suicide. But instead, the company's leaders are adding fuel to the fire.

Facebook's Network of Networks

On top of everything else, the team at MySpace should be particularly concerned about Facebook, the (relatively) new kid on the block. In fact, I suspect that by the time this book is published, Facebook will be the largest social network on the Internet, surpassing MySpace in users and page views.[21]

Like Microsoft, Facebook was started by a Harvard dropout. Founder Mark Zuckerberg wanted to connect with all of his Harvard classmates, and so he launched Facebook in February 2004.[22] It was a hybrid of Classmates.com and MySpace, except that Facebook was only for Harvard students. That very limitation made it a huge success: while MySpace was growing out of control, Facebook gave its Harvard users the control and community rarely seen in the larger social networks. Before the end of its first day, Facebook had registered twelve hundred Harvard students. By the end of its first month, more than half of Harvard's student body was online.[23]

That's when Zuckerberg took a risk. He quit Harvard, moved to Silicon Valley, and raised venture capital from Founder's Fund, the same group that started eBay's PayPal and Napster.[24] Starting with

Harvard, Facebook methodically enlarged its network to additional Ivy League schools, then to all colleges and universities, and then to all schools. Finally, Facebook opened to the world in September 2006.

By then, Yahoo reportedly had offered the twenty-two-year-old Zuckerberg nearly $1 billion for the company.[25] Most people thought Zuckerberg was nuts, but he turned Yahoo! down. Then Microsoft stepped up just as Facebook reached 30 million users and attained a growth rate that eclipsed every site on the Web except MySpace.[26] Microsoft bought less than 2 percent of the two-year-old company in 2007 for a reported $240 million (and for anyone having trouble with the math, that would value Facebook at roughly $15 billion).[27] Zuckerberg was not nuts (Microsoft, I am less sure of).

What I find interesting about Facebook is its resemblance to Jim Anderson's network of networks. Zuckerberg, like most entrepreneurs, stumbled on a model of the mind through trial and error instead of understanding the brain. Recall that Anderson realized that the brain is not as homogenous as researchers had once thought. On top of that, the number of neural connections is not very great. The average neuron has roughly 10,000 connections to other neurons in the brain. But the total potential connections is about 10^{10} (100,000,000,000). In other words, actual connectivity is only about 0.0001 percent of what it could be.[28]

But Jim's model assumes that neural activity is not evenly distributed. Instead, the network of the brain is built on clusters of neurons, each tightly connected within itself. These clusters then connect to other clusters and eventually form one network composed of many subnetworks—a network of networks. The beauty of this model (figure 9-1 represents the model introduced

FIGURE 9-1

Network of networks modular architecture

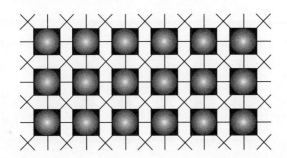

Source: Courtesy of James Anderson.

in figure 1-3), is that the brain allows the overall network to grow while maintaining equilibrium within its subnetworks.

Many things grow in this same way. Consider, for example, the infrastructure of a highway. Within cities there are many roads, and they are very well connected. But there are fewer roads that go across cities or travel long distances. What you have is a network of networks that creates (or enables) population density to increase and improves the flow of traffic within the overall network (see figure 9-2).

The same model applies to the Internet. The hardware of the Internet—computers—is connected through fiber optics and cable. These connections are not evenly distributed. Instead, clusters of computers are tightly connected (for example, computers in an office intranet), and the clusters are then loosely connected through the Internet to other clusters (see figure 9-3).

The same is true for Web sites. Researchers have analyzed connections among Web sites and found that they tend to create

FIGURE 9-2

A network of networks enables population density and improves traffic flow

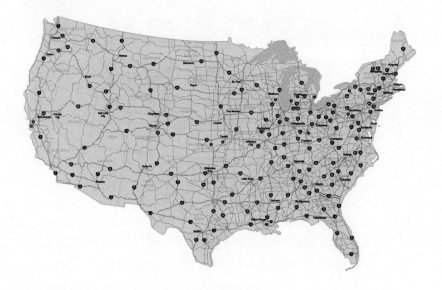

Source: Copyright 2008 Jupiter Images Corporation.

tightly connected Web sites within clusters that are only loosely connected to other clusters of tightly connected Web sites.

Take a step back and compare figures 9-1 through 9-3: it is astounding how similar they are.

The genius of Facebook, then, can be found in its network-of-networks approach. As Facebook evolves, it continues to create internal points of equilibrium within subnetworks, which it calls "groups" or (no surprise) "networks." As the company notes, "Facebook is made up of many networks, each based around a workplace, region, high school or college."[29] Each of these networks is tightly connected, in the sense that each has many users that have strong connections to one another. Across those

FIGURE 9-3

Clusters of computers connect to other clusters in the Internet

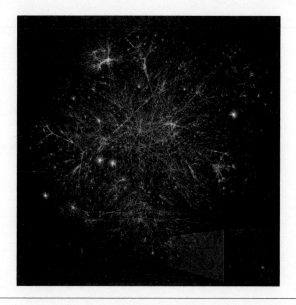

networks, however, the user relationships are more sparse (just as the brain's neurons link mostly to those neurons within their subnetworks). For Facebook, this arrangement started in a controlled way—first with Harvard, then to other schools, and finally to corporations. But as Facebook opened to the world, these clusters continued to proliferate, because Facebook encouraged users to subscribe to subnetworks (see figure 9-4).

The greatest advantage of the network-of-networks approach is the ability it gives Facebook to continue to enlarge the overall network while maintaining equilibriums within the subnetworks. There are other advantages as well. One of MySpace's problems, you may recall, was the randomness of the connections; anyone could connect to anyone else, even pedophiles to children. The

FIGURE 9-4

Clusters of Web sites are connected to clusters of other Web sites

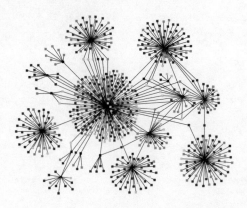

Source: Adapted from http://prblog.typepad.com/strategic_public_relation/images/2007/06/22/simple_social_network.png.

network-of-networks approach helps solve this problem. Facebook leverages existing associations to control the risk of out-of-network associations.

As one of the leading online social networking news sites described it, "A big difference on Facebook is that the friends you add are usually your real friends. It's not a contest like on MySpace where everyone is trying to have the most friends. On Facebook it is about talking to the people you know and sharing things with them . . . Both sites have groups, but Facebook makes them more prominent."[30] With Facebook, you focus on your friends within your networks, and not on the overall social network.

But Facebook is not immune to the tugging and pulling of the Internet economy. Despite the protection of the network of networks approach, out-of-network expansion still happens. With more than 100 million users at last count, the dangers that have affected MySpace affect Facebook as well.[31] In fact, Facebook now has its own chief privacy officer.[32] It has also signed a pact with attorneys general in various states to implement features to thwart predators, stalkers, and scammers.[33] But even with Facebook's growth approaching that of MySpace, those issues of unwanted solicitation are not nearly as severe.

The real issue is whether Facebook can hold true to its network-of-networks approach. Remember that the brain as a whole eventually reaches a period of equilibrium. After this comes a massive implosion. In a recent issue of *The Economist*, Facebook's "in-house sociologist," Cameron Marlow, acknowledged that the average user only has about 120 friends, of which only 7–10 are close friends.[34] This corresponds closely with two phenomena of the brain: first, the Dunbar number, a limit of roughly 150 on the brain's capacity for relationships; and second, Miller's magic number 7 ($\pm$2), which as we discussed earlier, is the capacity of short-term memory.[35] So what is Facebook facing? If we observe the brain, the answer is clear.

Will the Internet Implode?

We've seen plenty of Web sites go down by becoming too big. All networks, even the Internet, at some point stop growing. But a more macro question is this: could the entire Internet implode? Again, I call upon Bob Metcalfe (Bob, please excuse me for using you once again as a straw man).

In 1995, Metcalfe made a bold prediction: "I predict the Internet . . . will soon go spectacularly supernova and in 1996 catastrophically collapse."[36] This, from Metcalfe of all people—one of the early inventors of the infrastructure of the Internet, the CEO of 3Com, and the namesake of the networking law "Bigger is better." Why was Metcalfe now saying that the Internet, one of the largest networks on Earth, was going to implode?

It turns out that in the early days of the World Wide Web, there were looming issues. Metcalfe based his prediction on four fundamental problems, all linked to the exponential growth of the Internet. First was that during peak times, the Internet was regularly losing 10 percent of its data and communication.[37] Imagine trying to listen to someone who leaves out one word in ten every time she opens her mouth. Second and third were problems with hardware and software, respectively. Because the Internet was still in its infancy, Metcalfe argued that buggy systems were likely to cause massive problems. Finally, he was concerned about global terrorism, the kind that comes in the form of viruses.[38]

And there were signs that the Internet was having its share of problems. Most alarming was that global outages were rampant. Consider America Online, at the time the largest Internet service provider. By 1994 AOL was openly admitting that it could not handle the load or demand of the Internet. It had started limiting the number of users online during peak times, almost begging customers to switch to competitors.[39] The problems culminated in August 1996 with a massive outage that affected six million AOL users.[40] By 1997, AOL was forced to refund millions of dollars to angry users who had sued over the problems.[41]

In another, more alarming incident that same year, a corrupt database rendered the World Wide Web virtually useless: e-mail was shut down, and domain names could be accessed only by using their numeric alternative.[42] Imagine having to visit Yahoo! by typing "69.147.76.15."

The Internet Is Dead; Long Live the Internet

But as we all know, the Internet did not catastrophically collapse and Metcalfe had to eat his words. It turned out that the Internet was far more resilient than many people had thought. More important, the Internet became stronger and more ubiquitous with each failure. What did not kill the Internet made it stronger.

But Metcalfe was not entirely wrong (he rarely is); he just missed the scope, timing, and significance of the collapse. The Internet does have its share of problems. Networking bottlenecks, loopholes, software bugs, viruses, computer glitches, and many other concerns have caused downtimes that lead many observers to believe that the Internet will one day implode. This fear caused the U.S. government to announce in 2008 a plan to reduce the Internet's external connections (or ports) from more than four thousand to fewer than one hundred to curb the cyber threat to national security, in what Secretary of Homeland Security Michael Chertoff called the Internet's "Manhattan Project."[43]

But all these problems, even the viruses, haven't destroyed the Internet. And in many cases, after a brief and painful period, the Internet grew stronger. After America Online's problems, more ISPs—including NetZero and Juno—sprouted up, offering increasingly better reliability. Broadband began to have increasing penetration, allowing more users to reach the Internet faster. Access became quicker, faster, and cheaper.

The Internet Corporation for Assigned Names and Numbers (ICANN) was formed in 1998 as a nonprofit dedicated to preserving the independence and reliability of the domain name system. It quickly eliminated many loopholes, such as the database problems that rendered domain names useless in 1997.

But people continue to debate the "inevitable" collapse of the Internet.[44] Each time a new pundit declares the Internet dead, the problems we face are always far greater than those that fueled previous fears. But it is because the Internet advances significantly each time it encounters and solves fundamental (or for the naysayers, fatal) flaws. When Metcalfe first made his prediction, the problem was simply the number of users coming online, primarily to gain access to e-mail. That problem caused issues, but, just as Metcalfe avowed would happen, the Internet proved resilient.

Soon after that, we saw concerns about the millennium, and the millennium came and went. Then came the flood of concerns about viruses and e-mail spam. Paradoxically, this problem propelled us to new heights with viral marketing and social networks. More recently came the flood of rich media, such as YouTube, which now processes more information than the entire Internet did in 2000.[45] That problem, too, will surely be solved, but there will be others. The point is that with each new problem comes a solution and a stronger Internet as a result.

So Metcalfe was right in a way; the Internet does have its problems. But his prediction was dead wrong: a catastrophic collapse has not happened. Instead, the Internet has evolved into something far more powerful. Remember when I said that Metcalfe had to eat his words? He did so, literally. In true stoic fashion, Metcalfe put his article into a blender and drank the milky paste during a well-attended Internet conference in 1996.[46]

PART IV

I, Internet

CHAPTER 10

The New Rules
of the Brain, Business,
and Beyond

HOW MUCH OF YOUR brain do you actually use? Most people say 10 percent—that's the popular answer.[1]

In a recent study, even college psychology students thought that we use only 10 percent of our brains.[2] Perhaps they had read William James, the venerable psychologist who said about the brain that "we are making use of only a small part of our possible mental and physical resources."[3] Or maybe they read that Albert Einstein and Margaret Mead held similar views.[4] Maybe they read the preface to Dale Carnegie's 1936 book *How to Win Friends and Influence People*, in which famed explorer Lowell Thomas stated, "Professor William James of Harvard used to say that the average person develops only 10 percent of his latent mental ability."[5] All these statements may well be correct, but none of them really addresses the question.

So what is the answer? It turns out that you use 100 percent of your brain virtually all the time. Even while you sleep, the brain is highly active. As neurologist Barry Gordon, from Johns Hopkins School of Medicine, explains, "We use virtually every part of the brain . . . the brain is active almost all the time."[6]

Indeed, while you may be concentrating on one task (such as trying to answer this question), you are simultaneously doing many others (such as sitting up, reading, focusing, and breathing). All these functions require brain activity. You may have seen a brain scan at some point that showed a certain area of the brain "lit up" with activity. Brain scans are often highlighted to show particular activity, but this is a bit deceiving because it causes people to think that the rest of the brain is not active. Overall, brain scans demonstrate that the brain is fully "lit" (see figure 10-1).[7]

The human brain does not have unlimited potential, at least not in the sense that our minds are limitless or underutilized. But in another sense, the brain is unbounded because we can leapfrog natural evolution by developing tools that expand our intellect beyond the mind. The Internet is the ultimate creation in that regard. That is why the Internet will work its way into every corner of our lives, connecting ever more closely to the things we do.

Think about how a mom and pop bicycle shop currently uses the Internet. Jan Thomson owns Jacksonville Bikes in Florida, and she uses the Internet to send e-mail, search for things, buy inventory,

FIGURE 10-1

The brain is normally fully active, even though brain scans may highlight specific tasks

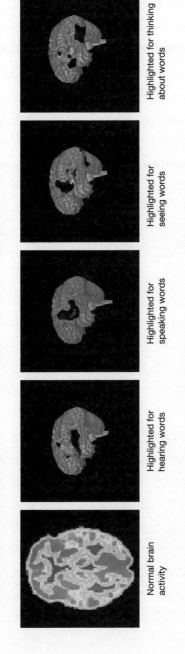

Normal brain activity

Highlighted for hearing words

Highlighted for speaking words

Highlighted for seeing words

Highlighted for thinking about words

Source: Courtesy of the Alzheimer's Disease Education and Referral Center, a service of the National Institute on Aging.

and advertise.[8] But as the Internet and the brain converge, the Internet will play an even larger role in her small business.

As a result of its prediction capacity, for example, a more personalized Internet will emerge. Eventually, as Internet applications get to know the "real you," the Internet will begin to tailor its offerings, enabling highly personalized reviews and information. Better predictions will help Jan of Jacksonville Bikes bring in more customers and match each one to the best bike. The Internet will help her review any customer feedback and compare it with sites the customer has visited as well as those of others with similar interests. It will quickly match demographic, psychographic, and behavioral information. And it will compare that data with the expert advice from Jan, along with the thoughts of the customer. All this will help match a customer looking for a mountain bike to the perfect carbon-fiber Kestrel, and someone looking for a ten-speed to an ideal Schwinn Continental with quick-release wheels and center-pull brakes.

What is happening to the Internet will have a direct impact on businesses, and nowhere is this more pronounced than in the ability of the Internet to learn to interpret, guess, and make predictions. As you saw earlier with the Netflix Prize, both the brain and the Internet are prediction machines. The Internet will advance far in this direction. As a result, the Internet will get better at interpreting subjective thoughts and opinions. Based on very little context from a new film, one day Netflix will be able to form an opinion and interpret people's thoughts. It will be able to alter its reviews based on input and responses. Or it may hold fast to its original "opinion." No matter how the Internet behaves, it will get increasingly better at making predictions, and this capability will enable businesses to do a better job serving their customers.

Big Brother

This is only a small fraction of the potential impact a more intelligent Internet will have on business. Yet even that impact is great. The Internet will also change society in profound ways. Imagine what will happen when the Internet starts to create sites independent of human programming. When you think about how much the Internet truly knows about you (search habits, purchase behavior, Web-surfing patterns), the thought is exhilarating.

Or frightening. In an article in the *New York Times*, reporters described using unidentified log files (surfing data) from AOL to determine exactly who was doing the surfing.[9] In one case, they were able to match "user number 4417149" to Thelma Arnold of Lilburn, Georgia, by looking at her "anonymous" search data.

Search data isn't really anonymous, despite what Google or AOL might lead you to believe. In the case of Thelma, she had searched on "landscapers in Lilburn, GA," "Arnold," "homes sold in shadow lake subdivision Gwinnett county Georgia," "60s single men," "numb fingers," "dry mouth," "thyroid," "dog that urinates on everything," and "swing sets." As the reporters put it, "search by search, click by click, the identity of AOL user No. 4417149 became easier to discern." And it didn't take the reporters much time to track her "anonymous" search files directly to Thelma. You can imagine Thelma's surprise, though, when she opened her door to find a reporter from the *New York Times* asking whether she had been able to get the dog pee out of her carpet last week. Yes, we have lost our privacy online.

But the positive benefits far outweigh the negatives. Think for a moment what a more personalized, dynamic Internet might look like. You might have your own personal advisory Web site based on everything from astrological charts to real-time weather forecasts (and, through biosensors, those forecasts would focus on where you are in the world). Or it might provide maps that predict where you might go and suggest the best routes. It might suggest book, music, or movie downloads for an upcoming plane ride that you booked through Expedia, optimizing based on the length of the anticipated trip or whether it is for personal or business purposes. One day, it might even build unique content tailored specifically for you, a Mad Libs for adults.

Once the Internet understands your entertainment habits, it could create custom books based on a subject you're interested in; original pieces of music based on your listening habits or your iTunes library; visually stimulating videos created from a library of images based on your mood and the time of day. Companies are already creating personalized Web sites that pull from available content based on download habits, information stored on your computer, and information gathered from your social and business networks. So all this is closer than you think and well ahead of current recommendation engines.

Medical companies like WebMD will evolve to become more interactive. The experience will be more like being in a doctor's office, with the patient being asked a series of symptomatic questions and offered medical advice. People will have their own virtual doctors, who will come to know them and their medical histories as well as their real doctors do. Imagine what that could do for the medical field and the cost of insurance.

These sites might take things a bit further and offer a personalized auto alert on, say, a tomato-borne *E. coli* scare, narrowing the information down to specific geographies and stores you frequent that are recalling the product (or notifying you as you sit down at your favorite Italian restaurant). The U.S. Centers for Disease Control are already using the Internet to track airborne viruses. A recent study showed that you can track flu and other disease outbreaks simply by following Internet searches.[10] It is not a giant leap to start using that information to help prevent the spread of those diseases.

In general, business ideas will emerge and evolve to reduce the complexity and stress of a hurried and busy lifestyle.

The Power of Thought

How will the Internet make our brains more powerful? To answer that, I return to the topic of the book's preface: BrainGate. Recall that with BrainGate, computer chips are being implanted into people's brains, giving them the power to control electrical devices and computers using nothing more than their thoughts. Companies like BrainGate are actively trying to link our brains to the Internet.

A number of companies are now doing this with video games. A company called Emotiv has a wearable helmet that uses EEG (a technical name for electrodes that are stuck to your forehead) to measure brain waves.[11] Emotiv uses those brain waves to interface with online games. Imagine playing Pacman with your mind; that is what the founders of Emotiv envisioned and are now implementing.

Zeo, a company that I helped start, has a wearable EEG headband that measures brain waves.[12] Its first product is an alarm clock that wakes you up in the earliest stage of sleep so that you don't feel groggy in the morning. As the *Boston Globe* put it, "Rather than waking you up at a precise time—say, 6:30 a.m.—the headband would monitor your brain waves using special sensors, and wake you up sometime in the half-hour leading up to 6:30 when you were in a light phase of sleep, which is preferable to being jolted out of deep sleep."[13] But it is more than that. Zeo also acts as an online sleep coach, recording data, providing you with a sleep score, and comparing your sleep patterns to those of others.

The problem in each of these cases, though, is that the technology is external and so the brain waves that are being measured are sparse. For Zeo, our feedback is "good enough" for an alarm clock and other consumer products. For Emotiv, the limited input from the brain is not sufficient, so it is supplemented with face and eye recognition.

But BrainGate is different. At roughly one-third the size of a penny, our implantable device directly attaches to neurons in the motor cortex of the brain. It uses one hundred electrodes roughly the width of a human hair to record brain activity across a small number of neurons. Although BrainGate requires brain surgery, the performance is like nothing before seen. Once the device is implanted, people are able to literally turn thoughts into action. As CNN reported in 2004 when our first microchip was implanted into the brain of a twenty-five-year-old quadriplegic man, "He can . . . turn lights on and off and control a television, all while talking and moving his head."[14]

Once you have an implanted device like this, the limits of the human brain become unbounded. In many ways, you are freed from the limitations of your body. You can connect your brain to the Internet, to a robot, or to a bionic arm. BrainGate could as easily be used to control a nuclear submarine as a wheelchair or a car. As a *Wired* reporter remarked after spending time with the first BrainGate patient, "In theory, once you can control a computer cursor, you can do anything from drawing circles to piloting a battleship."[15]

As with any great innovation, the lines of science and science fiction are being blurred. There is now a real possibility of downloading "memory implants" or retrieving information wirelessly from the Internet.[16] Recall that the Google founders envisioned a future with "the entirety of the world's information as just one of our thoughts." We may be getting a bit ahead of ourselves, but that future may become a reality with BrainGate.

This technology has the potential to be revolutionary for those who are severely disabled. It will enable bionics, restore speech, and give disabled people unimaginable access to a world that the able-bodied take for granted. How will BrainGate change the world for the rest of us? I can't say, but it is fun to imagine.

CHAPTER 11

A Ghost on the Web

WHAT DO UNDERAGE girls have to do with New York's governor? More important, what do they have to do with millions of Yahoo! readers? That's what a lot of people wondered when Yahoo! posted a news article about the disgraced Eliot Spitzer's dalliance with prostitutes—and then offered its audience a link to more information, including photos of "underage girls."

Big problem.

The problem originated with a predictive intelligence technology that Yahoo! had developed called Shortcuts. With Shortcuts, Yahoo! highlighted certain words in news stories and automatically linked them to popular searches. Unfortunately, Shortcuts learned more about human nature than we might want it to know—specifically, that many searchers on the Web are look-ing for a specific thing called sex. So Shortcuts, being naïve and immature, made the logical leap: because the Spitzer news story was about sex and happened to include the unfortunate combina-tion of words *underage girls*, Shortcuts figured that readers would enjoy similar stories, pictures, and Web sites.[1] The average child might make the same leap, if it were not for the fact that it would mean a leap off a socially unacceptable cliff.

In the end, Yahoo! did what any self-respecting company would do: it reined in Shortcuts and blocked the offending phrase from its vocabulary—never to be uttered again.[2]

Swipey-Wipies and Swirly-Whirlies

If the Internet is a brain, is it simply a reflection of ourselves? If it is, then sex is certainly on our minds, as it is in abundance online. Why should it shock us to see the Internet, or what amounts to a growing brain, imitating what we think inside our heads?

Just like the human brain, the Internet will make innocent blunders (as poor Shortcuts did). In the 1950s and 1960s, Art Lin-kletter's TV show *Kids Say the Darndest Things* depended for its humor on this aspect of human nature. It was easy to laugh—somewhat nervously—hearing stories such as this one: "One sum-mer evening during a violent thunderstorm a mother was tucking her son into bed. She was about to turn off the lights when he asked with a tremor in his voice, 'Mommy, will you sleep with me tonight?' The mother smiled and gave him a reassuring hug. 'I can't, dear,' she said. 'I have to sleep in Daddy's room.' A long silence was broken at last by the boy's shaky little voice: 'The big sissy.'"

We see these blunders in the innocent expressions of children every day. During the recent wildfires in California, one family that fled the flames said that their two-year-old continued to repeat, "Home. Home. Home." And in her sleep, she kept murmuring, "No fire. No fire. No fire."[3] Again, we see a developing brain putting together the patterns of human intelligence.

I recently took my three-year-old son to the Jacksonville Zoo. A highlight of this award-winning zoo is an animal train that takes children and adults on a ride through the caged animal kingdom. As we traveled along the tracks, my son pointed out all the animals he knew. He showed me monkeys, giraffes, and elephants less than gleefully enjoying their surroundings. But then things took a turn for the unexpected. My son started interweaving other things into his tour: "There's a gorilla, a back-hoe loader, a penguin, and a swipey-wipey."

Before you call child services on me, a "swipey-wipey" is what he calls the flapping squeegee devices in a car wash (these round squishy rollers are apparently called "swirly-whirlies"), which were being used to create a windbreaker in the lion's den. So that wasn't what I found strange.

What surprised me was how quick my son was to group trucks and swipey-wipies into the same category as animals. I asked him why he brought them up, and he said that they were in the zoo and part of the tour. He fully believed they belonged there, just as the animals did. More to the point, he saw them as exactly the same as the animals, no different in any respect. Machines as well as animals moved, were happy, were playful, and ate food (albeit neither hay nor gas seemed particularly tasty to my son).

It turns out that this line of thinking is not unusual, and I of all people should have realized it. In graduate school my research showed, among other things, that adults—arguably intelligent adults from Brown University—felt quite natural about categorizing things based on whether or not they are animated. In fact, these students were happy to put machines in the same category as animals, just as my three-year-old son had done at the zoo. A moving machine is considered more similar to an animal than is a rock or a fork or a toaster. But a turnip is considered more similar to a rock than to an animal. The Brown students intuitively knew better, but they couldn't resist the temptation to categorize based on animation.[4] Unlike my son, I suspect that they do not believe that a back-hoe loader can think, feel, and graze in the grass. But the Latin root for *animate*, it turns out, is "soul," so maybe my son has it closer than the Brown students.

Ghost in the Machine

If we are willing to categorize machines and animals together, then what makes us think that we cannot create a machine that thinks like an animal? And if an animal, why not a human?

No less a thinker than Descartes fell prey to this dilemma. He was actually of the same belief as my son and the Brown students: Descartes was convinced that animals were merely machines with soft furry outsides. I guess you could say he had the mind of a three-year-old, except that he was one of the greatest thinkers of all time.

Descartes realized that the brain was a machine (my son would never have figured this out) but couldn't see how the brain could be the thing in our heads doing the thinking. So he invented another concept, that of the mind. It is the mind—and not the brain—said Descartes, that makes us who we are. And what is this thing that he called the mind? It was an unknown supernatural phenomenon, no different from an elusive "ghost in a machine."[5] But if you have learned one thing from this book, it is this: there is no ghost, no ethereal mind, no magical goo in our brains. The brain is a machine that thinks.

Some of what I have discussed in this book scares people. The thought that the brain is a machine (and that as a result something other than humans can be intelligent) seems frightening. Whether it be Martians invading our planet, apes talking back to us, a ghost in a machine, or the Internet recommending underage girls, it is easier to call it all science fiction.

But nonhuman intelligence is already among us. It's true. Bees and ants have a social capacity that far exceeds that of humans in many ways (researchers at Stanford have shown that colonies collaborate and communicate in ways that approximate neurons in the brain).[6] Chimpanzees have been known to use complex tools.[7] Gorillas have been trained to use sign language. Koko, a famous gorilla (if a gorilla can be called famous), can understand more than two thousand words and once asked for a dentist because of a toothache.[8] Elephants, with their peanut-sized brains, can recognize themselves in mirrors, a sure sign of self-awareness.[9] And who has not loved a cat or dog? Can you say they are not intelligent?

Charting the Course

So what does this mean? In many ways, it's hard to say. It would be like asking Christopher Columbus, when he set his flag on the island of Hispaniola, "So what does this mean?" He couldn't have answered. (Of course, when he went back to Spain, he came up with a plausible report for the queen, but that's because otherwise he risked imprisonment or beheading.) Even the great thinker Steven Pinker doesn't have an answer. When asked what it would mean to wire up a billion Chinese people to simulate the neural connections of a brain (academics!), he replied, at a level of honesty rarely heard in the academic or scientific realm, "It beats the heck out of me."[10]

Still, many people make predictions about the future. No one is more bold or outspoken than Ray Kurzweil. He is no high-tech ingénue. Kurzweil invented the flatbed scanner and—after a meeting with little Stevie Wonder (he was still "little Stevie Wonder" back then)—also invented the first device to read books for the blind, along with the voice synthesizer to turn the print in those books into speech. (Kurzweil later invented the musical synthesizer: remember the Paul McCartney/Stevie Wonder hit "Ebony and Ivory?" That's Ray's synthesizer at work.) Kurzweil was named inventor of the year by MIT and the Boston Museum of Science. He is a member of the U.S. Patent Office National Inventors Hall of Fame and has been given the National Medal of Technology.[11]

What does Kurzweil predict for the future? (Queue the flashback music.) "It is now 2019 . . . a $1,000 computing device is now approximately equal to the computational ability of the human brain . . . the vast majority of transactions now include a simulated person . . . there are widespread reports of computers passing the Turing test [for intelligence] . . ."[12]

And by 2029? Kurzweil predicts that we will be saying that "a $1,000 unit of computation has the computing capacity of approximately 1,000 human brains . . . Automated agents are now learning on their own . . . significant knowledge is being created by machines with little or no human intervention . . . The majority of human communication does not involve a human being. The majority of communication involving a human is between a human and a machine."[13]

Is Kurzweil on target? I don't know. He is a braver man than I am. He's smart, too: when he made these predictions in 1998, he said of 2009 that personal computers with high-resolution visual displays would come in a range of sizes (think iPhones); cables would be disappearing (think Wi-Fi); purchases and reservations would take place with a virtual personality (think Expedia and Amazon.com); intelligent courseware would emerge as a common means of learning (think online education, such as University of Phoenix); accelerating returns from the advance of computer technology would result in continued economic expansion (true, at least until recently); and human musicians would routinely jam with "cybernetic" musicians (think Rockstar and Guitar Hero).[14]

So is Kurzweil right about 2019, 2029, and the future of artificial intelligence? Of course, I can't be sure. The frailty in all human foresight is that we extrapolate from what we know, and that practice sometimes leads us way off the mark. That said, I wouldn't bet against him, and many of his thoughts have been echoed throughout this book.

The Gravity of the System

Kurzweil was concerned mainly with computers, but the Internet, as you have seen, is fundamentally different. The question is, then, where is the Internet heading. Considering that Bob Metcalfe offered to eat a copy of his predictions (and subsequently put them in a blender and did so), I'll make the same bet. What the heck, paper is only fiber, and we all need more fiber in our diet— right?

And luckily for me, in the case of the Internet we have the brain as a guide, so there are some clues that can be drawn from nature. As a baby's brain develops, there is an explosion of neural development. And we are seeing a flood of new Web sites come online to our baby brain. In the early days of the Internet, there was a combinatorial explosion of new Web sites, but that has slowed over the past few years.

The Internet has passed through its early embryonic stage. Web sites continue to be built but at much slower rates. But those sites have increasing numbers of links to each other, mimicking the way a newborn starts to explore the world and build causal relationships that translate into neural and semantic connections. Given the way search engines spider and rank Web sites, there is a strong incentive to increase the number of links, and that is propelling development forward (and by accident or design, those spiders were made to monitor the activity of a baby brain).

The Internet may be a baby brain now, but it won't be for long. The Internet is growing at a mind-numbingly fast rate. Like a growing brain, link relevance is becoming more important, Web sites are decaying and dying (the technical term for this is *deprovisioning*, and the business term is *churn*). Links that have no traffic or usefulness are disappearing from Web sites.

Eventually, Internet algorithms will mature and, like the brain, start discounting, discarding, and penalizing links that are irrelevant, unnatural, or fake. At some point, the Web itself, through one of its governing bodies (the CIAs of the Web: W3C or ICANN) may even take action and proactively remove bad links. We will see a constriction at some point of Web sites as well as links, because such limits are central to an evolutionary path that remains "fast and frugal."

Other, more revolutionary changes will occur. William James, who may as well have been the only psychologist, given his influence on the field, said, "There is no cell or group of cells in the brain of such anatomical or functional preeminence as to appear to be the keystone or gravity of the whole system."[15] But this is the opposite of what the Web has evolved into. You learned earlier that neurons are different from Web sites: whereas a neuron's power comes from the network of neurons it is connected to, an individual Web site can hold (in theory) infinite amounts of information. On the Internet, individual Web sites are the gravity of the whole system.

But this situation will change as the Internet matures into an adult brain. Although Web sites store information, their power, too, lies in the ways in which they connect to one another. A network of sites creates a density of content, relevance, and independence that no individual site can seize, just as a catalytic converter is far more powerful in the context of a combustion engine. But this horsepower cannot be used . . . yet.

As the Web evolves, the value of these networks of networks will increase: new programs, algorithms, spiders, and frameworks will be developed to leverage that power. In the near future, Web sites will pull information from various sites to create collages of new information; search engines will leverage link structure to determine category information and not only popularity; the Web itself will enable the formation of content clusters that will in turn enable a semantic Web; and increasingly complex neural networks will evolve that will allow for communication, networking, and thought.

Equally important, the underlying structure of links on the Web will change. Currently, links have one dimension: the royal blue connections from one site to another. But that is not how the brain works. The brain has two types of links: inbound (axons) and outbound (dendrites). Memories are even richer in their semantic links (i.e., a 911 is a Porsche; a Porsche is a fast car; fast cars get more speeding tickets; speeding tickets and fast cars cost a lot of money). The Web will evolve to incorporate richer links and relationships. Sites will need to display the links that are coming in, and that will provide a proxy for what the site is about.

Neurons also weight their links, and this is reflected in the relative strengths of memories, but that does not happen on the Web. Internet links will evolve to incorporate weighting, allowing everyone to see how relevant and important a link is on a given page. Think of it as a color code, where blue might represent the best links on the page, red second best, yellow third, and so on. In the beginning, site owners may choose their most important links, but the system will evolve to allow dynamic weighting based on how many people click on each link or how relevant the link is.

The ultimate goal is that information will become as readily available as it is in our brains. We have no search engines in our minds. Instead, information spreads across a series of connected memories, links in our brains to other information—this is how we think. One day, entering thoughts, feelings, or aspirations into the Web will generate a similar process—it will open up endless information, dynamically organized based on your thoughts. Ultimately, this will render search engines (and yes, even Google) obsolete.

Sites will also become modular, enabling not only independent editors (as we now see at Wikipedia, where anyone can edit the online encyclopedia) but also the Web itself to modify the very sites that are a part of it. Just as the brain can modify memories and even create new ones, the Internet will be able to modify and create Web sites.[16] Sound strange? It shouldn't be hard to imagine, because it is already happening to some extent. A news report you saw on CNN.com may have been posted earlier on Reuters and picked up by millions of sites automatically, including CNN. And remember that the "underage girl" story on Yahoo! had dynamic links generated, not by CNN or even a Yahoo! editor, but by an algorithm on the Web. In the brain and on the Web, information is not static.

The brain is a sponge in that it soaks up information, but from that point, information is manipulated and integrated into the rest of the knowledge stored in the brain. In advertising, this means you need to position your message appropriately.[17] On the Internet, it means you must let go and be willing to let your information change and adapt as the social network reacts to it.

Looking ahead, new Web sites will be created that pull together clusters of information that are tightly linked. The network of networks that we find on Facebook will be applied to the Web. No longer will you need to go to a dozen car sites or an aggregator like Autobytel or even Google to find information about the best hybrid SUV. Instead, the Internet will create a page with only the most interesting and relevant information across the Net. Even today, there is a small start-up called Kosmix.com that is building what I call *dynamic portals*—search for anything and they return a page dynamically generated from content all over the Web. The Web will one day be able to generate a Web page specific to your request, just as the brain fires off new symphonies of excitation when it encounters a novel subject.

And what of Moore's and Metcalfe's laws? They will both peter out under the weight of their own gravitational force. This should not be surprising, because all exponential growth eventually stalls. But what does that say for computers and the Internet? My prediction is that it will fuel a new era of productivity in which software advances will outpace the growth we've seen in hardware; intelligence will emerge, not from brute force but from educated guesses. Remember that the brain is a slow computer, so we do not gain intelligence from sheer size or speed. What makes us smart is that we are loopy, slow, and speculative. When the Internet can no longer count on productivity gains from brute force, it will turn to other measures, and that will surely come from mimicking the power of the brain.

Collective Consciousness

The shift from hardware to software advances will drive us closer to intelligence and consciousness online. Perhaps we are getting ahead of ourselves, but not by much. Consider the new breed of virtual reality Web sites. Already some fifteen million people participate in Second Life, a site where they submerge themselves into cyberspace and become persons they are not in real life.[18] And Second Life is only one of about a dozen popular virtual reality worlds.

Will virtual reality, then, be the intelligence behind the Internet? Rather than an extension of human thought, will it come in the form of some kind of ingestion of human intelligence within the framework of an artificial world? This would not be the first time that science fiction cut the path that reality was destined to follow.

What if the lines become blurred? Will we be unaware of the intersection between minds and machines?[19] Consider the story of a robbery that happened in 2007. Days after the robbery, police in Amsterdam were told the story of a woman who had started a furniture store on Humbolt Street three years earlier and had a thriving business until someone broke in and stole $4,000 worth of furniture. The police were given an unusual amount of detail, so they were confident that justice would be served.

The police began their investigation and quickly learned a few odd facts. First, Humbolt Street isn't in Amsterdam or even in the Netherlands. What's more, the thieves couldn't be found anywhere.

The reason, as it turned out, is that the crime didn't happen in Amsterdam or even in "this world." It happened in Habbo Hotel, a virtual world that exists only on the Internet. But the crime was real, and the furniture, while virtual, cost real Euros. And here is where things get strange: the Dutch police agreed. They ended up pursuing the case, finding the virtual thieves (in the real world), and arresting them. The thieves have been banned from the virtual world and will likely serve time in a real jail.[20]

What is happening in virtual life is merely an extension of real life—or in some cases a replacement. Hundreds of thousands of people now gladly give up their Saturday evenings to go on dates in a virtual world, such as Habbo Hotel or Second Life. Habbo now claims to have more than eighty million people in thirty-one countries; it is a busy hotel, to say the least.[21] And that is dwarfed by Second Life's vibrant marketplace, which transacts as much as 100 million real U.S. dollars per year and is minting real millionaires.[22] The people in these virtual worlds are having real interactions, exchanging real money, and living real lives, albeit in a virtual world.

It makes one wonder whether the body (sitting in front of a keyboard for hours) is nothing more than a brain on life support—Descartes' ghost. Earlier in my career, I had just that experience: I would spend hours in a cubicle on the phone with various people, some of whom I got to know quite well. But at one point, I had an eerie feeling that I was nothing more than a brain, floating in space, communicating with other brains. (Not to worry—my wife cured me with a few beers.)

Many people end up with this feeling, and often they experience a backlash against technology. With radio, there were the dangerous frequency waves. Television introduced many evils: ADD, brain cancer, desensitization, cultural vacuums. Do cell phones cause cancer, or only make us less personable? For every paperless office and electronic book, there are people touting the value of the printed word. What will become of the Internet when the pundits declare it too dangerous, too malicious, or even too smart?

That is a question we will soon face, because an intelligent Internet is imminent. It will not resemble a brain, I'm certain, any more than the first airplane flapped its wings like a bird. But like an airplane, the intelligence behind the Internet will go faster and farther than what has preceded it on Earth. If we consider that only sixty-six years after the first flight of the Wright brothers, astronauts set foot on the moon, what does that say for the future of the Internet? The Internet has already given us opportunities that far exceed the impact of flight, but that is nothing compared with what is coming. It's a bit scary, I admit. And if you think that the idea of an intelligent Internet is unsettling, what about one that is self-aware?

I Think, Therefore I Am the Internet

In the next sixty-six years, it is hard to say where we will be. Will the Internet be talking back to us? Probably, as text-to-speech software continues to improve. Will it be better at making decisions than it is now? Certainly, as we have already seen the success that many companies have had with prediction algorithms. Will the Internet be embedded in our minds through a BrainGate, as I discussed earlier? That could be, at least for some brave souls.

But what about the million-dollar question: will "The Internet" be conscious? And will it have feelings, needs, desires? Could it be that the Internet will wake up one day, seek out the prettiest girl, and ask to touch her mammary glands? That's unlikely if you think about the way the Internet is developing.

Remember that we are comparing the Internet to a brain, not an individual human being. So let's not measure the Internet by the "yardstick of our own years."[23] Brains can be used for many things, and they can even be shared (whether it be by conjoined twins or by colonies of bees and ants). It is unlikely that Google's cloud will become "The Internet" and wake up one day and wonder whether it is going to rain. Nor is it likely to gain control of "The Internet" and strike thunderous vengeance on Microsoft's or Amazon.com's cloud. And don't expect "The Internet" to feel pain or love or dream or understand the world around it. That is not what will happen to "The Internet." Rest assured, "The Internet" will not gain consciousness.

But that does not rule out consciousness on the Internet. On the contrary, it is far more likely that we will see multiple personalities on the Web. You should expect certain systems on the Internet to reach the level of consciousness that we reserve only for the smartest of animals, including humans.[24] John Markoff of the *New York Times* wrote a few years ago, "From the billions of documents that form the World Wide Web and the links that weave them together, computer scientists and a growing collection of start-up companies are finding new ways to mine human intelligence."[25] A number of companies are building software that leverages the brain to create what we think of as human consciousness.

For example, brain scientist Doug Lenat has been working on a "mechanical brain" for the past twenty years that re-creates all the world's information.[26] His project is called CYC, and he started it by inputting large databases of information by hand but has now moved on to the Web. His goal is to teach CYC common sense—in other words, how to laugh, cry, love, and interpret the world. As for consciousness, Lenat says, "I think it's conscious now."[27]

I could go on ad nauseam, because pondering the future of a conscious Internet is almost endless. But allow me instead to leave you with this one thought from—who else?—Dan Dennett:

> Here's a little fantasy to scare you. A virus lands on the planet and begins to take over and grow and grow and grow, and it needs us to provide it with energy and repair, but it provides us with lots of services that we like, and it gradually makes us more and more dependent on it, to the point where we realize that many of the things that we hold most dear we can no longer accomplish without feeding this virus and helping it grow until it finally takes over the planet. Now that's a pretty scary scenario, and it's not true, in one regard, in that the virus did not come from outer space. It's called the information superstructure of the world or the web, internet, and it's already here, and we are already dependent on it. So, it's too late to go back. We're going to have to maintain whatever control we can over it and that control is already beginning to slip.[28]

I agree with Dennett. I think it's already here. But it's not a bad thing. It's going to be fun—and pretty exciting.[29]

The Brain of the
New Machine

O N A ROUTINELY sunny afternoon in Sunnyvale, California, a green Mustang convertible pulled into the parking lot of one of the many mirror-glassed corporate offices that line Highway 101. Sunnyvale and its neighboring urban villages are home to some of the most amazing inventions of our time. Within a twenty-five-mile circumference, inventors have created the semiconductor, the vacuum tube, the integrated circuit, the personal computer, and more. A new breed of even more competitive high-tech innovators is pushing the boundaries even further.

It was for this reason that the young man, as he approached the building, had to go through an elaborate security check. Because it was a Saturday, the check went quickly. He rode up the elevator into a vast space filled with identical-looking cubicles. His cubicle had the requisite pictures of his girlfriend and parents, plus dog. The horseshoe-shaped desk was cluttered with books and papers; the two big computer screens were alive with tropical fish awaiting a more important task.

He sat down and began to type rapidly on the keyboard. It was as though he was unleashing ideas that had stormed around in his mind that night—thoughts that he had held in abeyance until he could get back to work. Now what looked like a vast network of electrical wiring appeared on the screen. Grasping the computer mouse, he moved a few of the branches around. Then he sat back and pondered what he had done.

His thoughts reeled back to his undergraduate years at the Universitá di Roma, where he had studied the philosophy of mind, and to his time at Brown University, where he had studied linguistics, neuroscience, and artificial intelligence.

The brain, he knew, looked like the images shown in figure E-1.

He returned his fingers to the keyboard. Now he brought up an image of the Internet. What he saw is shown in figure E-2.

He knew from his graduate studies that the similarities between the images were more than happenstance: he was looking at two brains, one more primitive than the other but nonetheless a brain. He began to type again, more rapidly now.

Had you been standing in the parking lot looking up at the curved glass building, you would have seen him there. The afternoon light was dimming into evening, lights were coming on in the office, the name of Internet titan Yahoo! was glowing bright purple over the highway. (Of course, intelligence on the Web

FIGURE E-1

The human brain and the Internet

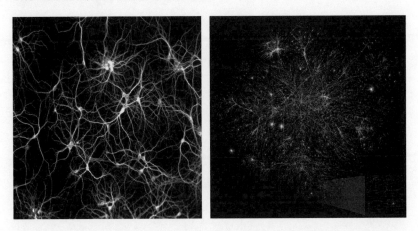

Source: Image (at left) courtesy of Paul De Koninck, www.greenspine.ca; image (at right) courtesy of the Opte Project through the Creative Commons license, http://creativecommons.org/licenses/by-nc-sa/1.0/.

moves quickly, so if you go to look for him now, you will find him at Google.)

This young man is not a figment of my imagination, not a fictional character. He is a friend and colleague, and one of many high-tech entrepreneurs looking for the connection between the Internet and the brain.[1]

Preface

1. For more on Einstein's mistakes, see Hans C. Ohanian, *Einstein's Mistakes: The Human Failings of Genius* (New York: W.W. Norton, 2008); for Edison's, see Harold Evans, "Edison's 2,998 Mistakes," *Los Angeles Times*, November 1, 2004, and Neil Baldwin, *Edison: Inventing the Century* (Chicago: University of Chicago Press, 1995); for more on Fleming's discovery of penicillin, see Kendall Haven, *Marvels of Science: 50 Fascinating 5-Minute Reads* (Westport, CT: Libraries Unlimited, 1994); for more on Viagra and failures that turn into successes, see Henry Chesbrough, "Managing Your False Negatives," *Harvard Management Update* 8, no. 8 (August 2003).

2. David Sheff, "Playboy Interview: Google Guys," *Playboy*, September 2004.

3. The company raised $5 million from Oxford Bioscience Partners in 2002, and an additional $4.3 million from the same source in 2003.

4. The company was called Cyberkenetics, but my team has since taken the BrainGate intellectual property private under a new company called BrainGate, Co.

5. Brown University, "Pilot Study of Mind-to-Movement Device Shows Early Promise," Press Release, March 2002.

6. L. R. Hochberg, M. D. Serruya, G. M. Friehs, J. A. Mukand, M. Saleh, A. H. Caplan, A. Branner, D. Chen, R. D. Penn, and J. P. Donoghue, "Neuronal Ensemble Control of Prosthetic Devices by a Human with Tetraplegia," *Nature* 442, no. 7099 (2006): 164–171; and M. D. Serruya, N. G. Hatsopoulos, L. Paninski, M. R. Fellows, and J. P. Donoghue, "Instant Neural Control of a Movement Signal," *Nature* 416 (2002): 141–142.

7. BrainGate is what John Brockman, founder of *Edge*, calls a dangerous idea: a scientific discovery that could send ripples through our moral and belief structures. Originally coined by philosopher Dan Dennett in *Darwin's Dangerous Idea: Evolution and the Meanings of Life* (New York: Simon and Schuster, 1995), the term was brought to Brockman's attention by Harvard psychologist Steven Pinker, who posed his "dangerous idea" in an *Edge* article. The topic was later

turned into a book—see John Brockman, *What Is Your Dangerous Idea? Today's Leading Thinkers on the Unthinkable* (New York: HarperCollins, 2007)—that included the dangerous ideas of nearly thirty leading scientists. In many ways, the book you're reading imparts my "dangerous idea."

8. "Harnessing the Power of the Brain," *60 Minutes*, November 2, 2008.

Introduction

1. Steven Pinker, *How the Mind Works* (New York: W. W. Norton & Company, 1999), 22.

2. The notion that we start out as empty vessels is an old one, and it continues to be held by many people. John Locke, with his *tabula rasa* theory, is often credited with this idea, but it dates to the ancient Greeks. For a poignant and accurate attack on Locke's *tabula rasa* see Steven Pinker, *The Blank Slate: The Modern Denial of Human Nature* (New York: Penguin Group, 2002). Or for the more daring, drop a baby head first into water (they instinctively hold their breath).

3. The term *encephalization* refers to the amount of brain mass relative to an animal's size and weight. It is generally believed that the greater the encephalization, the greater the intelligence of a species. Humans, to no surprise, have virtually the highest amount of encephalization (particularly as it relates to the cerebral cortex) in the animal kingdom. This was recognized by Darwin, who wrote in *The Descent of Man,* "No one, I presume, doubts that the large proportion which the size of man's brain bears to his body, compared to the same proportion in the gorilla or orangutan, is closely connected with his mental powers." For more on the Great Encephalization, see Daniel C. Dennett, *Darwin's Dangerous Idea: Evolution and the Meanings of Life* (New York: Simon & Schuster, 1996).

4. Michael Woods, *Ancient Construction*, (NY, NY: Twenty-First Century Books, 2000), 37

5. The Internet was created by a U.S. government defense agency called ARPA (Advanced Research Projects Agency), which provides research grants for many new scientific and technology innovations. The initial Internet—called ARPANET—was a link between Stanford (SRI) and UCLA in 1969. ARPANET moved slowly from there: in 1981, there were only 213 total connections.

6. Edward O'Neill, Brian Lavoie, and Rick Bennett, "Trends in the Evolution of the Public Web 1998–2002," *D-Lib Magazine*, April 2003.

7. David A. Vise and Mark Malseed, *The Google Story* (New York: Bantam Dell Publishing Group, 2005), 78.

8. For a great debate on the subject in general, see Steven Pinker and Jacques Mehler, eds., *Connections and Symbols: A Cognition Special Issue* (Amsterdam: Elsevier Science Publishers, 1988). As will be clear, even people in the same field have sharp disagreements on how the mind works.

9. Daniel C. Dennett, *Consciousness Explained* (New York: Little Brown & Co., 1991).

Chapter 1

1. Howard Margolis, *Patterns, Thinking, and Cognition: A Theory of Judgment* (Chicago: University of Chicago Press, 1988), 60.

2. There are two types of mentors: those who spend endless time with you and become trusted confidants; and those who offer sage advice that changes your life. For me, Dan is the latter. The little time I spent with him, the few words he spoke, were powerful. I came to him originally to study philosophy. Instead of welcoming me, he encouraged me to go off and study science and then come back to philosophy after I had "experience." That advice turned me on to brain science and psychology, something that ultimately led me back to philosophy, as Dan had suspected.

3. Daniel C. Dennett, *Consciousness Explained* (New York: Little Brown & Co., 1991), 27.

4. Ibid., 29.

5. Ibid., 268.

6. Ibid., 189–190.

7. Also see Douglas R. Hofstadter and Daniel C. Dennett, eds., *The Mind's I: Fantasies and Reflections on Self and Soul* (New York: Basic Books, 1981).

8. Dennett, *Consciousness Explained*, 189–190.

9. Eric Clapton, *Clapton: The Autobiography* (New York: Broadway Books, 2007), 29.

10. See Jeffrey Stibel, "Increasing Productivity through Framing Effects for Interactive Consumer Choice," *Cognition, Technology & Work* 7, no. 1 (March 2005): 63–68.

11. James A. Anderson, Paul Allopenna, Gerald S. Guralnik, David Sheinberg, John A. Santini Jr., Socrates Dimitriadi, Benjamin B. Machta, and Brian T. Merritt, "Programming a Parallel Computer: The Ersatz Brain Project," *Studies in Computational Intelligence (SCI)* 63 (2007): 61–98.

12. It is worth also checking out Jeff Hawkins, my second favorite neuron hunter. Jeff was the founder of Palm Pilot and Handspring, but his true passion was neuroscience. He wrote a great book on intelligence—titled, no surprise, *On Intelligence* (New York: Times Books, 2004)—and recently started a neuroscience institute and a company (Nuementa) based on his vision for creating machine intelligence.

13. V. B. Mountcastle, "Introduction," *Cerebral Cortex* 13 (January 2003): 2–4.

14. Anderson et al., "Programming a Parallel Computer: The Ersatz Brain Project," 63.

Chapter 2

1. "Inside the World of Google The Dalles," *(Dalles) Chronicle,* August 5, 2007.

2. For a remarkable overview of cloud computing, see George Gilder, "The Information Factories," *Wired*, October 2006.

3. For more on Bisciglia and an excellent description of the Google facility, see Stephen Baker, "Google and the Wisdom of Clouds," *BusinessWeek*, December 13, 2007.

4. Ibid.

5. Ibid.

6. Ben Franklin said this in April 1778, almost one hundred years before Darwin's *On the Origin of Species*.

7. Richard Dawkins, *The Selfish Gene* (Oxford: Oxford University Press, 1989).

8. Ibid., 206.

9. André Leroi-Gourhan, *Gesture and Speech*, trans. A. Bostock Berger (Cambridge, MA: MIT Press, 1993), 236.

10. Clayton M. Christensen, *The Innovator's Dilemma: The Revolutionary Book That Will Change the Way You Do Business* (Boston: Harvard Business School Press, 1997).

11. Thomas Kuhn, in *Structure of Scientific Revolutions* (Chicago: University of Chicago Press, 1996), put forth a theory of nonlinear evolution for scientific discoveries, where a brazen scientist upends history by proving that an established paradigm is in fact wrong; Clayton Christensen did the same for business in *The Innovator's Dilemma*.

12. Richard Dawkins, *A Devil's Chaplain: Reflections on Hope, Lies, Science, and Love* (New York: Houghton Mifflin, 2003), 28.

13. Read Montague, *Your Brain Is (Almost) Perfect: How We Make Decisions* (New York: Penguin Group, 2006), 200.

14. Steven Pinker, *How the Mind Works* (New York: W. W. Norton & Company, 1999), 67.

15. Von Neumann's proposal for the EDVAC can be read at http://qss.stanford.edu/~godfrey/vonNeumann/vnedvac.pdf.

16. Ray Kurzweil, *The Age of Spiritual Machines: When Computers Exceed Human Intelligence* (New York: Penguin Group, 1999), 25.

17. Gilder, "The Information Factories."

18. Urs Hölzle, in a speech at CERN, reported in "A Search Engine That's Becoming an Inventor," *New York Times*, July 3, 2006.

19. Jeffrey Dean and Sanjay Ghemawat, "MapReduce: Simplified Data Processing on Large Clusters," *Communications of the ACM* 51, no. 1 (January 2008): 107–113.

20. Ibid.

21. Mark Horowitz, "Visualizing Big Data: Bar Charts for Words," *Wired*, June 23, 2008.

22. Years before Google's cloud, in fact, a company that United Online purchased did just this. Juno, a large Internet service provider (ISP) similar to AOL,

built a massively parallel computing cloud using idle computers on the Internet, creating what was the largest supercomputer in history. For a review of Juno's supercomputing cloud, see "Juno to Harvest Wasted PC Power," Associated Press, February 1, 2001.

23. Quoted in Gilder, "The Information Factories."

24. Quoted in "A Search Engine That's Becoming an Inventor."

Chapter 3

1. www.netflix.com.

2. See www.netflixprize.com; Jordan Ellenberg, *Wired*, "This Psychologist May Outsmart the Math Brains," February 25, 2008; and David Leonhardt, *New York Times*, "You Want Innovation? Offer a Prize," January 31, 2007.

3. Gerd Gigerenzer, *Gut Feelings: The Intelligence of the Unconscious* (New York: Penguin Books, 2007), 4.

4. Elkhonon Goldberg, *The Wisdom Paradox: How Your Mind Can Grow Stronger as Your Brain Grows Older* (London: The Free Press, 2005), 9.

5. Ibid., 48.

6. R. Maex, Erik De Schutter, "Resonant Synchronization in Heterogeneous Networks of Inhibitory Neurons," *The Journal of Neuroscience*, November 19, 2003, 23(33)

7. Daniel C. Dennett, *Consciousness Explained* (New York: Little Brown & Co., 1991)

8. Ibid., 177.

9. Montague, *The Brain is (Almost) Perfect*, 83.

10. Steven Pinker, "Yes, Genes Can Be Selfish," *The Times* (London), *March 2006*, <http://www.timesonline.co.uk/tol/news/uk/science/article736740.ece>

11. Pinker, *How the Mind Works*, 30.

12. Daniel Goleman, *Emotional Intelligence* (New York: Bantam Books, 1995), 15.

13. Ibid., 17.

14. James P. Hogan, *Mind Matters: Exploring the World of Artificial Intelligence* (New York: Del Rey/Ballantine, 1997), 119.

15. Ibid., 71.

16. Ibid., 65.

17. For other examples, see S. A. Sloman, David Over, Lila Slovak, and J. M. Stibel, "Frequency Illusions and Other Fallacies," *Organizational Behavior and Human Decision Processes* 91, no. 2 (2003): 296–309.

18. Dan Ariely, *Predictably Irrational: The Hidden Forces That Shape Our Decisions* (New York: HarperCollins, 2008).

19. Nassim Taleb, *The Black Swan: The Impact of the Highly Improbable* (New York: Random House, 2007).

20. Stephen Jay Gould, *Full House* (New York: Three Rivers Press, 1996), 96. Gould also talks about "the myth of progress," and, seeing what is happening in the financial markets of 2009, I must sadly agree.

Chapter 4

1. Herbert Simon, *Administrative Behavior* (New York: Free Press, 1947).

2. For a fascinating and in-depth description of Simon, see James P. Hogan, *Mind Matters: Exploring the World of Artificial Intelligence* (New York: Del Rey/Ballantine, 1997).

3. For details, see ibid., 119.

4. Henry Allen, "Gammonoid the Conqueror," *Washington Post*, July 17, 1979, B1.

5. Quoted in Stuart Russell and Peter Norvig, *Artificial Intelligence: A Modern Approach* (New York: Prentice-Hall, 1995), 20.

6. Cited in Michael Zey, *The Future Factor: Forces Transforming Human Destiny* (Piscataway, NJ: Transaction Publishers, 2004), xx.

7. Malcolm Gladwell, *Blink: The Power of Thinking Without Thinking* (New York: Little, Brown and Company, 2005), 255.

8. Ibid., 256.

9. These articles by Gigerenzer include a few contradicting my graduate research, but let's not hold that against him (heck, he was probably right).

10. Gerd Gigerenzer, *Gut Feelings: The Intelligence of the Unconscious* (New York: Viking, 2007), 151.

11. Quoted in Gladwell, *Blink: The Power of Thinking Without Thinking*, 255; 300.

12. A. See Jeffrey Stibel, Itiel Dror, and Talia Ben-Zeev, "The Collapsing Choice Theory: Dissociating Choice and Judgment in Decision Making," *Theory and Decision* 66, no. 2 (2009): 149–179.

13. B. Tversky and D. Kahneman, "Extension Versus Intuitive Reasoning: The Conjunction Fallacy in Probability Judgment," *Psychological Review* 90, no. 4 (October 1983): 293–315. For a general overview of the field see D. Kahneman, P. Slovic, and A. Tversky (eds.), *Judgment Under Uncertainty: Heuristics and Biases* (Cambridge, UK: Cambridge University Press, 1982).

14. R. Hertwig and G. Gigerenzer, "The 'Conjunction Fallacy' Revisited: How Intelligent Inferences Look Like Reasoning Errors," *Journal of Behavioral Decision Making* 12 (1999): 275–305; for a general overview see G. Gigerenzer, P. M. Todd, and the ABC Research Group, *Simple Heuristics That Make Us Smart* (New York: Oxford University Press, 1999).

15. S. A. Sloman, David Over, Lila Slovak, and J. M. Stibel, "Frequency Illusions and Other Fallacies," *Organizational Behavior and Human Decision Processes* 91, no. 2 (2003): 296–309.

16. Dan came up with the idea for "exploding coupons," wherein you have a limited time—say, five seconds—to purchase something at a steep discount. He also helped create Amazon.com's Gold Box, which presents relevant products at a discount but only for a short period.

17. Johnson interview at Amazon.com (http://www.amazon.de/exec/ obidos/ tg/feature/-/217324/ref%3Ded_cp_le_1_4/302-1180530-0945615). See also Steven Johnson, *Emergence: The Connected Lives of Ants, Brains, Cities, and Software* (New York: Touchstone, 2001). See also Johnson, *Mind Wide Open: Your Brain and the Neuroscience of Everyday Life* (New York: Scribner, 2004).

18. Chris Anderson, "The Zen of Jeff Bezos," *Wired,* January 2005.

Chapter 5

1. Associated Press, "Amazing Memory Man Never Forgets," republished at CNN.com/health, February 22, 2008.

2. Elkhonon Goldberg, *The Wisdom Paradox* (New York: Gotham Books, 2005), 108. Writes Goldberg, "Memories for trivial, inconsequential events continue to decay very rapidly every hour following the events, and this decay is characterized by a steep power function. And thank God for that."

3. Associated Press, "Amazing Memory Man Never Forgets."

4. Goldberg, *The Wisdom Paradox*, 109.

5. For a fascinating and provocative overview, see Eric Kandel, *In Search of Memory* (New York: Norton and Co., 2006).

6. Joseph A. Schumpeter, *The Theory of Economic Development: An Inquiry into Profits, Capital, Credit, Interest and the Business Cycle* (Cambridge: Cambridge University Press, 1934).

7. Clayton M. Christensen, *The Innovator's Dilemma: The Revolutionary Book That Will Change the Way You Do Business* (Boston: Harvard Business School Press, 1997). It is interesting to note that Schumpeter talks about "nonrational innovations." These seem to be exactly the innovations done "less well" that Christensen speaks of. See, for instance, J. A. Schumpeter, *The Theory of Economic Development: An Inquiry into Profits, Capital, Credit, Interest and the Business Cycle* (Cambridge, UK: Cambridge University Press, 1934).

8. Christensen, *The Innovator's Dilemma*, 10.

9. Stephen Jay Gould, *Full House: The Spread of Excellence from Plato to Darwin* (New York: Three Rivers Press, 1997).

10. To be fair, we recently hired a president who has an extensive marketing background. In fact, both the CEO and the president came from United Online, where they helped market the Juno, NetZero, and Classmates.com brands. But the type of marketing they do online is very different from anything they have done before.

11. Both NetZero and Juno were great turnaround stories. The companies were considered to have inferior products when our team, led by turnaround expert Mark Goldston, merged the two companies. At the time (early 2001), the combined company was worth $70 million. Three years later, it was worth over $1 billion and by 2008 had made approximately $800 million in adjusted profitability. For a great strategic review of turnarounds, see Mark Goldston, *The Turnaround Prescription* (New York: Free Press, 1992).

12. Many of these ideas are also illustrated in Geoffrey Moore's classic *Crossing the Chasm: Marketing and Selling High-Tech Products to Mainstream Customers* (New York: HarperCollins, 1991).

13. Caching is now a multibillion-dollar industry. You probably haven't heard their names, but companies such as Akamai Technologies, Limelight, and Edgecast now handle more than 15 percent of all traffic on the Internet. (In full disclosure, I serve on the board of Edgecast.)

14. The details are not particularly sexy, but the semantic Web has brought us things few people have heard of but many of us unknowingly use every day: XML, RDF, OWL, SPARQL, and RIF, languages that make the Web more rich and robust.

15. For a good overview of the Web 2.0 model, see Dan Tapscott and Anthony D. Williams, *Wikinomics: How Mass Collaboration Changes Everything* (New York: Penguin Group, 2006) or Charlene Li and Josh Bernoff, *Groundswell: Winning in a World Transformed by Social Technologies* (Boston: Harvard Business School Publishing, 2008).

16. Tim Berners-Lee and Mark Fischetti, *Weaving the Web* (San Francisco: HarperSanFrancisco, 1999), chapter 12.

Chapter 6

1. Hypertext was developed by Andries van Dam (a Brown professor of computer science) and inventor Ted Nelson.

2. Web sites, of course, are not analogous to neurons by any means. There are many ways in which neurons and Web sites are different: neurons have the ability to increase the strength (or weight) of their connections, but Web sites have only one dimension for linking (at least for now). Neurons can connect and grow without human intervention, but Web sites cannot evolve at all without assistance. Neurons are simple and stupid as individuals but grow infinitely more powerful as a network; that's not entirely so with Web sites. Neurons also have the unseemly trait of oozing chemicals, but Web sites don't.

3. Wim van den Dungen, "Neurophilosophical Inquiries," 2003, http://neuro. sofiatopia.org/brainmind.htm; and R. Joseph, *The Naked Neuron* (New York: Plenum Press, 1993); W. Howells, *Getting Here* (Washington, DC: Compass, 1992).

4. Netcraft, Netcraft 2008 Web Server Survey, http://news.netcraft.com/ archives/2008/12/index.html.

5. Daniel C. Dennett, *Consciousness Explained* (New York: Little Brown & Co., 1991).

6. See research by The Poynter Institute for a good overview and comparison of how we read Web sites versus newspapers For example, as opposed to what I described for Web sites above, people tend to read newspapers from top to bottom, without much scanning across the page. The most read parts of a Web page, in contrast, are the upper left, top, middle, left side, and right side, followed by the bottom of the page. Online, readers tend to scan Web pages for content before they dive in, and this pattern supports that. So online, readers scan the page—instead of methodically reading it like a newspaper—which means that content should be chunked into headlines and the most important information should follow the "hot zone" flow above. Poynter conducts annual eye-tracking studies and has extensive research on the subject.

7. Banner blindness is a very interesting psychological phenomenon on the Web. After years of seeing annoying, blinking banner ads, people unconsciously ignore the spaces where banners were most prevalent. The term was coined by two Rice University professors. See Jan Panero Benway and David M. Lane, "Banner Blindness: Web Searchers Often Miss 'Obvious' Links," *ITG Newsletter*, December 1998.

8. "Answers Corp. Buys Dictionary.com," TheStreet.com, July 16, 2007, http://www.thestreet.com/story/10368141/1/answers-corp-buys-dictionarycom.html.

9. ComScore Media Metrix, 2007.

10. "Answers.com Sees 28% Traffic Drop As Google Algorithm Changes; Will Dictionary.com Deal Go Through?" *Forbes*, August 2, 2007; and Om Malik, "Answers.com Raises Questions About Google's Power," August 2, 2007, http://gigaom.com/2007/08/02/answerscom-raises-questions-about-googles-power/.

11. Daniel C. Dennett, "Memes and the Exploitation of Imagination," *Journal of Aesthetics and Art Criticism* 48 (1990): 131. Reprinted five years later in Daniel C. Dennett, *Darwin's Dangerous Idea: Evolution and the Meanings of Life* (New York: Simon and Schuster, 1995). (The original quote substituted "vehicle" for "medium" but I prefer *medium* myself.)

Chapter 7

1. The conference, hosted by Infornortics, was "Search Engines Today and the New Frontier, The Fifth Search Engine Meeting."

2. Page did manage to make it on a panel discussion.

3. At one point, Larry and I had a heated discussion about the value of the size of a search engine versus its ability to index and rank results. We seemed to be the only two CEOs at the conference who were focused on the quality of results that appeared on the first page rather than how many results a search engine generated.

4. Terry Winograd, *Understanding Natural Language* (New York: Academic Press, 1972); Winograd, *Language as a Cognitive Process* (New York:

Addison-Wesley, 1983); Winograd, *Understanding Computers and Cognition: A New Foundation for Design* (New York: Addison-Wesley, 1987).

5. Simpli.com is now owned by a public advertising company called ValueClick. That company also owns my first patent for search engine interfaces.

6. It was George Miller who discovered that our ability to remember trivial things in short-term memory was limited to roughly seven pieces of information. This led to the phone system and many other innovations, all of them revolving around what George called the magic number 7. For one of the best written academic papers around, see George's graduate thesis: "The Magical Number Seven, Plus or Minus Two: Some Limits on Our Capacity for Processing Information," *Psychological Review* 63 (1956): 81–97.

7. For an excellent, although somewhat technical, review of WordNet, see Christiane Fellbaum, ed., *WordNet: An Electronic Lexical Database* (Cambridge, MA: MIT Press, 1978).

8. Steven Pinker, *How the Mind Works* (New York: W.W. Norton & Company, 1999), 14.

9. Daniel C. Dennett, *Consciousness Explained* (New York: Little Brown & Co., 1991), 58.

10. Allan M. Collins and Elizabeth F. Loftus, "A Spreading-Activation Theory of Semantic Processing," *Psychological Review* 82, No. 6 (November 1975): 407–428.

11. I owe most of this overview, as well as the overview of Zipf's law later in this chapter, to Jim Anderson, Paul Allopenna, Carl Dunham, Andrew Duchon, David Landan, John Santini, George Miller, Steve Reiss, Dan Ariely, and the entire brain science team at Simpli.com.

12. Stefanie Olsen, "Automated Search Ads Can Boomerang," *CNET News*, September 26, 2003.

13. The law was named after linguist George Kingsley Zipf who originally put forth the theory.

14. Chris Anderson, *The Long Tail: Why the Future of Business Is Selling Less of More*, revised and updated edition (New York: Hyperion, 2008).

15. McKinsey & Company, "Americans Received Six Billion Credit Card Offers Through Direct Mail," 2007.

16. Katie Hafner, "Google Options Make Masseuse a Multimillionaire," *New York Times*, November 12, 2007; Erick Schonfeld, "Counting the Google Millionaires," *TechCrunch*, November 12, 2007.

17. Compete.com annual survey, January 2007. Web sites that have overtaken their competitors typically have more unique users, and yet those users typically spend less time on the site itself. MySpace (11.9 percent of time online) and its newest competitor, Facebook (1 percent of time online), are good examples of this. For an interesting take on these statistics, read Bill Tancer's *Click* (NY: Hyperion, 2008). Bill works for Compete.com's competitor, HitWise (owned by Experian).

18. http://www.google.com/corporate/tech.html; and http://en.wikipedia.org/wiki/PageRank.

Chapter 8

1. George Gilder, "Metcalf's Law and Legacy," *Forbes ASAP,* September 13, 1993.

2. Al Gore, "Basic Principles for Building an Information Society," *USIA Electronic Journals* 1, no. 12 (September 1996).

3. http://en.wikipedia.org/wiki/Network_effect.

4. The only person who seemed to notice and fully understand what was happening was Yale economist Robert Schiller. On the eve of the bubble's bursting he published *Irrational Exuberance* (Princeton, NJ: Princeton University Press, 2000), outlining his theory and rationale and explaining why Metcalfe's law could not continue to sustain the Internet bubble.

5. Bob Metcalfe (guest blogger), "Framing the First Massachusetts Energy Summit," VCMike's Blog, December 16, 2006.

6. Don't confuse Metcalfe's law with Metcalfe's original idea. His law, coined and expanded on by others, may be wrong, but Metcalfe was correct in his original thinking.

7. John Dowling, *Creating Mind: How the Brain Works* (New York: W. W. Norton & Company, 1998), 124.

8. S. M. Blinkov and I. I. Glezer, *The Human Brain in Figures and Tables: A Quantitative Handbook* (New York: Plenum Press, 1968).

9. John Dowling, *The Great Brain Debate: Nature or Nurture?* (Princeton, NJ: Princeton University Press, 2007), 140.

10. For a great analysis of the Darwinian drive behind the neuron, see Gerald Edelman, *Neural Darwinism* (New York: Basic Books, 1987).

11. C. R. F. Brandão and D. Agosti, "The Ant Colony Cycle," American Museum of Natural History, January 3, 1998, http://research.amnh.org/entomology/social_insects/ants/ant_colony_cycle.html.

12. E. Strohm and A. Bordon-Hauser, "Advantages and Disadvantages of Large Colony Size in a Halictid Bee: The Queen's Perspective," *Behavioral Ecology* 14, no. 4 (May 2005): 546–553.

13. Stephen Budiansky, "The Physics of Gridlock: What Causes Traffic Jams? The Depressing Answer May Be Nothing at All," *Atlantic*, December 2000.

14. Steven Johnson, *Emergence: The Connected Lives of Ants, Brains, Cities, and Software* (New York: Scribner, 2001). Johnson's first diagram visually compares the human brain to a map of Hamburg, circa 1850. The similarities of the map are striking to the brain: it has networks of streets that mimic brain regions, a central artery of a river that flows out of what looks like a brain stem, regions that run parallel to brain hemispheres, and an outer perimeter similar in design to the

cerebral cortex. You can see a reproduction of that Hamburg map courtesy of Wikipedia at http://en.wikipedia.org/wiki/File:Map_hamburg_1800.png.

15. Ibid., 51, 146.

16. Quoted in ibid., 147.

17. Although Metcalfe's law may be incomplete, it does not mean that Metcalfe himself did not appreciate this. In a recent article, Metcalfe even hinted at our new law, encouraging his critics (of which I am not one) to take "another crack at my poor old law" and "look at whether the value of a network actually starts going down after some size." See Bob Metcalfe (guest blogger), "Metcalfe's Law Recourses Down the Long Tail of Social Networks," VCMike's Blog, August 18, 2006. Metcalfe clearly believed that there is (or may be) a point of diminishing returns past a certain point for a network. I am less sure whether he realized that, as a network stops growing, it paradoxically becomes more powerful.

18. University of Illinois at Urbana-Champaign, "The Brain Loses Neurons During Adolescence," *ScienceDaily*, March 19, 2007.

Chapter 9

1. For a good overview of Rosenblatt's career, see Erika Brown, "The Mixologist," *Forbes*, September 26, 2007. Or check out a recent issue of *Forbes*, where Rosenblatt was compared to Adrian Grenier (Vince Chase of HBO's *Entourage*).

2. SEC filing, Intermix Media/Inc., February 24, 2004.

3. MySpace was officially created by Chris DeWolf, Josh Berman, and Tom Anderson. The backstory is a bit more interesting, because quite a few others claim to be cofounders, including Brad Greenspan, ex-CEO of eUniverse. You can find all the gory details (or at least Greenspan's opinions) at www.freemyspace.com. Regarding Classmates.com, MySpace cofounder Chris DeWolfe recognizes Classmates.com as the original social network in a BBC interview, December 2006, http://news.bbc.co.uk/1/hi/programmes/click_online/6197914.stm.

4. Andrew Leonard, "You Are Who You Know," Salon.com, June 16, 2004.

5. Classmates.com was still a huge success for United Online, and it continues to be the company's biggest driver of growth, although by social networking standards that growth is relatively small, less than tripling within seven years. See Associated Press, "IPO Spotlight: Classmates Media," December 10, 2007.

6. Anita Hamilton, "100,000 Friends: On Friendster.com, Nobody's a Stranger for Long," *Time*, November 17, 2003; and "Breakouts 2003," *Entertainment Weekly*, December 12, 2003.

7. Max Chafkin, "How to Kill a Great Idea!" *Inc.*, June 2007.

8. Daniel Terdiman, "Friendster's Fakester Buddies," *Wired*, July 12, 2004.

9. "Attack of the Smartasses," *SF Weekly*, August 13, 2003.

10. Patricia Sellers, "MySpace Cowboys," *Fortune*, August 29, 2006.

11. Chafkin, "How to Kill a Great Idea!"

12. Pete Cashmore, "MySpace Hits 100 Million Accounts," Mashable.com, August 9, 2006.

13. For a good statistical overview of the various social networks, check out http://www.web-strategist.com/blog/2008/01/09/social-network-stats-facebook-myspace-reunion-jan-2008/.

14. Steve Rosenbush, "News Corp.'s Place in MySpace," *BusinessWeek*, July 19, 2005.

15. "Google Signs $900m News Corp Deal," BBC News, August 7, 2006.

16. Andrew Meyer, "News Corp: MySpace Worth $6 Billion," *TechCrunch*, November 15, 2006. One of the MySpace founders has argued that MySpace is worth more than $20 billion (see "MySpace Founder Seeks Inquiry: The Ousted Executive Says News Corp. 'Bilked' Investors Out of Billions in Its Deal for the Site," *Los Angeles Times*, October 6, 2006). For an interesting take on the MySpace follies, see Julia Angwin, "Stealing MySpace: The Battle to Control the Most Popular Website in America" 2009.

17. Kevin Poulsen, "Pillaged MySpace Photos Show Up in Massive BitTorrent Download," *Wired*, January 23, 2008.

18. Peter Kafka, "MySpace Clips Facebook in January, but Both Slowing," *Silicon Valley Insider*, February 11, 2008.

19. Even searching for uncommon names, such as Mary Lincoln, causes problems (five pages with more than five hundred names).

20. Chloe Albanesius, "MySpace, Attorneys General Target Online Predators," *PC Magazine*, January 14, 2008; you can view the report by the attorneys general at http://ago.mo.gov/newsreleases/2008/pdf/MySpace-JointStatement0108.pdf.

21. At the time this manuscript was submitted, Facebook had already surpassed MySpace. That was back in November 2008. And by the time the book was in editorial, Facebook director (and founder of Netscape) Marc Andreessen reported on February 22, 2009, during an interview on the *Charlie Rose Show*, that Facebook had surpassed 175 million users. The latest rumor is that Facebook has already surpassed 200 million users.

22. There are too many good articles about the history of Facebook to cite here. The best place to get a general overview is at Wikipedia.org/wiki/Facebook.

23. Sarah Phillips, "A Brief History of Facebook," *Guardian*, July 25, 2007.

24. For more on Founder's Fund, see www.foundersfund.com. The team has an impressive track record, including LinkedIn, PayPal, Friendster, Xoom.com, and Facebook.

25. Kevin Delaney, "Facebook, Riding a Web Trend, Flirts with a Big-Money Deal," *Wall Street Journal Online*, September 21, 2006, http://online.wsj.com/article/SB115880835590769754.html?mod=home_whats_news_us.

26. Pete Cashmore, "Facebook's Massive Growth: Hits 30 Million Active Users," Mashable.com, July 10, 2007.

27. Microsoft, "Facebook and Microsoft Expand Strategic Alliance," Press Release, October 24, 2007.

28. R. W. Williams and K. Herrup, "The Control of Neuron Number," *Annual Review of Neuroscience* 11 (1988): 423–453.

29. www.facebook.com/networks/networks.php.

30. Ben Gold, "Facebook Hammers MySpace on Key Features," Mashable.com, June 10, 2007.

31. Roddy Lindsay, "We're Making Lexicon Better," Facebook, news release, September 19, 2008. That number is now estimated to be over 200 million.

32. Anne Barnard, "Facebook Agrees to More Safeguards," *New York Times*, October 17, 2007.

33. Stephanie Reitz, Associated Press, "Facebook, States Set Predator Safeguards," May 8, 2008.

34. "Primates on Facebook," *The Economist*, February 26, 2009.

35. See R. I. M. Dunbar, "Neocortex Size as a Constraint on Group Size in Primates," *Journal of Human Evolution* 22 (1992): 469–493; or R.I.M. Dunbar, "Coevolution of Neocortical Size, Group Size And Language in Humans," *Behavioral and Brain Sciences* 16, no. 4 (1993): 681-735.

36. Bob Metcalfe, "From the Ether," *InfoWorld*, December 4, 1995.

37. Bob Metcalfe, "The Internet After the Fad," speech, University of Virginia, May 30, 1996, http://americanhistory.si.edu/collections/comphist/montic/met calfe.htm.

38. "Bob Metcalfe on What's Wrong with the Internet: It's the Economy, Stupid," *IEEE Internet Computing* 1, no. 2 (March 1997): 6–17. Viruses are a nuisance (as in the case of the Creeper, which simply sent a message stating, "Catch me if you can" in the 1970s), or they can do serious damage, as in the case of Melissa, which halted the entire Internet communications system in 1999. One of the worst viruses on record was the I Love You virus, which many of us remember from receiving an e-mail message of the same name that demonstrated anything but love. In the end, it took down the e-mail systems of the Pentagon, CIA, and British Parliament, shut down hundreds of companies' Web sites, destroyed and erased millions of documents, and cost the world economy an estimated $5 billion to $15 billion.

These viruses do so much damage because they self-replicate. Viruses jump from one computer to another across the Internet; they replicate, mutate, and spread like weeds across the Web. Richard Dawkins said that artificial life was possible years before the advent of viruses when he called computers "honorary living things." But it took viruses to convince the legions of biologists, such as John Maynard Smith, to believe in the possibility of "artificial evolution." Oxford biological anthropologist Robert Aunger—in the book *Electric Meme: A New Theory of How We Think* (New York: Free Press, 2002—goes so far as to say, "This is real evolution. It even involves replication" (119). In the early days, this prospect was so worrisome, not unlike Darwin's original theory, that Aunger recalls that "virus incidents were widely considered urban myth (like rumors of alligators in the sewers of New York)" (122).

39. Leslie Helm, "America Online Finds It Can't Handle the Load," *Los Angeles Times*, February 2, 1994.

40. Doug Abrahms, "Outage's Fallout Shows Just How On-line America Is," *Washington Times*, August 1996.

41. Steve Lohr, "Refunds Planned by America Online in Network Jam," *New York Times*, January 30, 1997.

42. Simson Garfinkel, "50 Ways to Crash the Net," *Wired,* August 19, 1997.

43. Ryan Singel, "U.S. Has Launched a Cyber Security 'Manhattan Project,' Homeland Security Chief Claims," *Wired*, April 8, 2008.

44. As of November 2008, I count twelve high-profile pundits and academics who believe that the Internet will collapse at some time between now and 2015.

45. Steve Lohr, "Video Road Hogs Stir Fear of Internet Traffic Jam," *New York Times*, March 13, 2008. Also see "Cisco, Approaching the Zettabyte Era," 6/08 or Mary Meeker's Morgan Stanley Tech Trends, March 2009, p. 47.

46. It occurred at the Sixth World Wide Web Conference, Santa Clara, California, on April 10, 1997.

Chapter 10

1. For an excellent review of this fascinating subject, see B. L. Beyerstein, "Whence Cometh the Myth That We Only Use 10% of Our Brains?" in *Mind Myths: Exploring Popular Assumptions about the Mind and Brain*, ed. S. DellaSala (Chichester: John Wiley and Sons, 1999), 3–24.

2. K. L. Higbee and S. L. Clay, "College Students' Beliefs in the Ten-Percent Myth," *Journal of Psychology* 132 (1998): 469–476.

3. William James, "The Energies of Men," *Science* 25, no. 635 (1907): 321–332.

4. Eric Chudler, "Myths About the Brain: 10 percent and Counting," University of Washington in Seattle, BrainConnection.com.

5. Quoted in Dale Carnegie, *How to Win Friends and Influence People* (New York: Simon and Schuster, 1936), 247–248.

6. Quoted in Robynne Boyde, "Do People Only Use 10 Percent of Their Brains?" *Scientific American*, February 7, 2008.

7. For a great review of the technology involved in brain scans and the underlying psychological mechanisms recorded, see Michael J. Posner and Marcus E. Raichle, *Images of Mind* (New York: Scientific American Library, 1994).

8. The company name and owner in this example are fictitious.

9. Michael Barbaro and Tom Zeller Jr., "A Face Is Exposed for AOL Searcher No. 4417749," *New York Times*, August 9, 2006. These thoughts are expanded in

Hal Abelson, Ken Ledeen, and Harry Lewis, *Blown to Bits: Your Life, Liberty, and Happiness After the Digital Explosion* (New York: Pearson Education, 2008).

10. http://blogs.wsj.com/health/2009/03/13/google-searches-as-early-warning-for-disease-outbreaks/?mod=yahoo_hs

11. Electroencephalography measures electrical activity in the brain and typically is used by doctors and researchers, but a number of budding entrepreneurs have found it useful for all kinds of fun things.

12. Zeo is a Brown University start-up founded by a handful of students. I was one of the founding board members, and Jim Anderson sits on our advisory board.

13. Scott Kirsner, "A Gentler Way to Start the Day," *Boston Globe*, March 28, 2005.

14. "Brain Chip Offers Hope for Paralyzed," CNN, October 21, 2004.

15. Richard Martin, "Mind Control," *Wired*, March 2005.

16. *gizmag* has a great piece on BrainGate that outlines the potential for memory implants (and describes the cautious optimism of the BrainGate team): "'BrainGate' Brain-Machine-Interface Takes Shape," *gizmag*, December 7, 2004, http://www.gizmag.com/go/3503/3/.

Chapter 11

1. The prostitute in question, however, was not underage, and Spitzer was never charged with a crime.

2. Michael Arrington, "Yahoo's Helpful Shortcut to Pictures of Underage Girls," TechCrunch, July 5, 2008.

3. Alex Gomez, "Wildfire Imperils Yosemite," *USA Today*, July 30, 2008.

4. J. S. Stibel, "The Role of Explanation in Categorization Decisions," *International Journal of Psychology* 41, no. 2 (2006).

5. "Ghost in the machine" was actually coined years later by renowned philosopher Gilbert Ryle, who provided a devastating critique of the notion that there is anything inside our heads other than a brain. Gilbert Ryle, *The Concept of Mind*, New University of Chicago Press edition (Chicago: University of Chicago Press, 2002 [1949]).

6. Deborah M. Gordon, Stanford University, (see http://www.stanford.edu/dept/news/pr/93/931115Arc3062.html).

7. For a good overview, see Constance Holden, "What's in a Chimp's Toolbox?" *Science*, October 7, 2004, 2.

8. "'Talking' Gorilla Demands Dentist," BBC News, August 9, 2004.

9. See Joshua M. Plotnik, Frans B. M. de Waal, and Diana Reiss, "Self-Recognition in an Asian Elephant," *Proceedings of the National Academy of Sciences* 103 (September 13, 2006): 17053–17057. It turns out that dolphins can also recognize themselves in mirrors. See Diana Reiss and Lori Marino, "Mirror Self-Recognition in the Bottlenose Dolphin: A Case of Cognitive Convergence," *Proceedings of the National Academy of Sciences* 98 (May 1, 2001): 5937–5942.

10. Steven Pinker, *How the Mind Works* (New York: W.W. Norton & Company, 1999), 146.

11. For a great biography of Kurzweil, just ask Ray: http://www.kurzweil tech.com/raybio.html.

12. Ray Kurzweil, *The Age of the Spiritual Machines* (New York: Penguin Books, 1999), 202–209.

13. Ibid., 220–224.

14. Ibid., 189–198.

15. William James, *The Principles of Psychology* (New York: Henry Holt and Company, 1981 [1890]), 180.

16. See, for example, Jeff Stibel, "The Internet & the Brain," http://blogs. harvardbusiness.org/stibel/. This *Harvard Business Review* article explains how thinking something can create the same memories as actually doing it.

17. See Al Reiss and Jack Trout, *Positioning: The Battle for Your Mind* (New York: McGraw-Hill, 2001 [1989]), for a classic argument for positioning messages in the brain.

18. "Second Life," Wikipedia, http://en.wikipedia.org/wiki/Second_Life.

19. In another real sense, cognition and technology are being blurred when it comes to how people are impacted by technology in general. As psychologist Itiel Dror has said, technology is "actively affecting and changing human cognition itself." See Itiel Dror, "Gold Mines and Land Mines in Cognitive Technologies," *Cognitive Technologies and the Pragmatics of Cognition*, ed. Itiel Dror (Amsterdam: John Benjamins, 2007), 1–2. See also Itiel E. *Dror* and Robin D. Thomas, "*The Cognitive Neuroscience Laboratory*: A Framework for the Science of Mind," in Christina E. Erneling and David Martel Johnson, eds., The Mind as a Scientific Object: Between Brain and Culture (New York: Oxford University Press. 2005), 283–292. For more details: http://www.ecs.soton or e-mail: id@ecs.soton.ac.uk. The entire book by Erneling and Johnson is fascinating.

20. See, for example, "'Virtual Theft' Leads to Arrest," BBC News, November 14, 2007.

21. Matt Chapman, "Dutch Teen Arrested for Habbo Hotel Thefts," iTnews, November 16, 2007.

22. Anshe Chung officially became the first Second Life millionaire in 2006 as a result of the value of her Second Life real estate holdings. See Rob Hof, "Second Life's First Millionaire," *BusinessWeek*, November 26, 2006.

23. This expression comes from a 1927 essay by W. Livingston Larned titled "Father Forgets," originally published in the now defunct *People's Home Journal*. In this wonderful piece, Larned realizes that he has been judging his son by the yardstick of his own years. I sneaked in the quote both because it is a timeless essay on fatherhood and because it is fitting as we look to a young and growing Internet.

24. There is no reason to think of this as dualism. Quite the contrary: I am not talking about homunculi here, but rather numerous entities emerging from the neural connectivity of a single, connected mind. There is some evidence that

this exists in nature. E. O. Wilson and his colleagues have been studying the behavior of ants for years and have demonstrated the ability of more than one "collective intelligence" to emerge from both individual ants and among colonies. See, for example, Edward O. Wilson, *The Insect Societies* (Cambridge, MA: Belknap Press of Harvard University Press, 1971); Bert Hölldobler and Edward O. Wilson, *The Ants* (Cambridge, MA: Belknap Press of Harvard University Press, 1990); Bert Hölldobler and Edward O. Wilson, The Superorganism: The Beauty, Elegance, and Strangeness Of Insect Societies (New York: W.W. Norton & Company, 2009).

25. John Markoff, "Entrepreneurs See a Web Guided by Common Sense," *New York Times*, November 11, 2006.

26. Doug and I had many conversations in 2000 about merging our two companies (Simpli.com and CYC). Nothing ever came of it, but in hindsight, it would have been a lot of fun to have worked with Doug.

27. Jeffrey Goldsmith, interview with Doug Lenat, "CYC-O," *Wired*, April 1994.

28. David G. Stork and Michael O Connell, "Evolution Intelligence: Daniel C. Dennett Interview," 2001: Hal's Legacy, www.2001halslegacy.com/interviews/dennett2.html.

29. For the more daring, I leave you with this quote: "[As] machines become more and more intelligent, people will let machines make more of their decisions for them, simply because machine-made decisions will bring better results than man-made ones. Eventually a stage may be reached at which the decisions necessary to keep the system running will be so complex that human beings will be incapable of making them intelligently. At this stage the machines will be in effective control. People won't be able to just turn the machines off, because they will be so dependent on them that turning them off would amount to suicide." This comes from Ted Kaczynski (the Unabomber) in *Unabomber Manifesto* (Nicholas Carr, *The Big Switch: Rewiring the World, from Edison to Google* (New York: W.W. Norton, 2008). Sometimes the lines are blurred between genius and insanity . . . And yes, my editor warned me not to end my book with a quote from the Unabomber.

Epilogue

1. His name is Massimiliano (Massi) Ciaramita. He is a friend of mine, and he helped start Simpli.com with me while we were both at Brown. I have taken some liberty here—for instance, I don't really know that his rental car in Sunnyvale was a green Mustang. In November 2008, Massi left Yahoo! to join Google in its Zurich research center.

BIBLIOGRAPHY

Abelson, Hal, Ken Ledeen, and Harry Lewis. *Blown to Bits: Your Life, Liberty, and Happiness After the Digital Explosion.* Upper Saddle River, NJ: Addison-Wesley Professional, 2008.

Anderson, C. *The Long Tail: Why the Future of Business is Selling Less of More.* New York: Hyperion, 2006.

Anderson, J. A. *An Introduction to Neural Networks.* Cambridge, MA: MIT Press, 1995.

Anderson, J A., and E. Rosenfeld. *Talking Nets: An Oral History of Neural Network Research.* Cambridge, MA: MIT Press, 1998.

Anderson, J. A., P. Allopenna, G. S. Guralnik, D. Sheinberg, J. A. Santini Jr., S. Dimitriadis, B. B. Machta, and B. T. Merritt. "Programming a Parallel Computer: The Ersatz Brain Project." *Studies in Computational Intelligence* 63 (2007): 61–98.

Anderson, J. R. *The Adaptive Character of Thought.* Hillside, NJ: Erlbaum, 1990.

Ariely, D. *Predictably Irrational: The Hidden Forces That Shape Our Decisions.* New York: Harper Collins, 2008.

Aunger, R. *The Electric Meme: A New Theory of How We Think.* New York: The Free Press, 2002.

Baldwin, N. *Edison: Inventing the Century.* New York: Hyperion Books, 1996.

Bar-Hillel, M., and E. Neter. "How Alike Is It Versus How Likely Is It: A Disjunction Fallacy in Probability Judgments." *Journal of Personality and Social Psychology* 65 (1993): 1119–1131.

Barabási, A-L. *Linked: How Everything Is Connected to Everything Else and What It Means for Business, Science, and Everyday Life.* New York: Penguin, 2002.

Benway, J. P. "Banner Blindness: The Irony of Attention Grabbing on the World Wide Web." *Proceedings of the Human Factors and Ergonomics Society Annual Meeting* 1 (1998): 463–467.

Benway, J. P., and David M. Lane, "Banner Blindness: Web Searchers Often Miss 'Obvious' Links." *Internetworking* 1.3, 1998.

Berners-Lee, T., with M. Fischetti. *Weaving the Web: The Original Design and Ultimate Destiny of the World Wide Web By Its Inventor*. San Francisco: HarperSanFrancisco, 1999.

Blinkov, S. M., and I. I. Glezer, *The Human Brain in Figures and Tables. A Quantitative Handbook*. New York: Plenum Press, 1968.

Bloom, P. "Intention, History, and Artifact Concepts." *Cognition* 60 (1996): 1–29.

Brafman, O., and R. Brafman. *Sway: The Irresistible Pull of Irrational Behavior*. New York: Doubleday, 2008.

Brockman, J., ed. *What Is Your Dangerous Idea? Today's Leading Thinkers on the Unthinkable*. New York: Harper, 2007.

Carnegie, D. *How to Win Friends and Influence People*. New York: Simon and Schuster, 1936.

Carr, N. *The Big Switch: Rewiring the World, from Edison to Google*. New York: W. W. Norton, 2008.

Chesbrough, H. "Managing False Negatives." *Harvard Management Update* 8, no.8, 2003.

Christensen, C. M. *The Innovator's Dilemma: When New Technologies Cause Great Firms to Fail.* New York: HarperBusiness Essentials, 2003.

Chu, C-T., S. K. Kim, Y-A. Lin, Y-Y. Yu, G. Bradski, A. Y. Ng, and K. Olukotun. "Map-Reduce for Machine Learning on Multicore." *Advances in Neural Information Processing Systems*, 19 (2007): 281–288.

Clapton, E. *Clapton: The Autobiography*. New York: Broadway Books, 2007.

Collins, A. M., and E. F. Loftus "A Spreading–Activation Theory of Semantic Processing." *Psychological Review*, 82 (1975): 407–428.

Collins, J. C., and J. I. Porras. *Built to Last: Successful Habits of Visionary Companies.* New York: Harper Business, 1994.

Cosmides, L., and J. Tooby, "Are Humans Good Intuitive Statisticians After All? Rethinking Some Conclusions from the Literature On Judgment Under Uncertainty." *Cognition* 58 (1996): 1–73.

Damasio, A. R. *Looking for Spinoza: Joy, Sorrow, and the Feeling Brain*. Orlando, FL: Harcourt, 2003.

Darwin, C. *On the Origin of Species by Means of Natural Selection, or the Preservation of Favoured Races in the Struggle for Life*. London: John Murray, 1859.

———. *The Descent of Man, and Selection in Relation to Sex*. London: John Murray, 1871.

Dawkins, R. *The Selfish Gene*. Oxford: Oxford University Press, 1976.

———. *A Devil's Chaplain: Reflections of Hope, Lies, Science, and Love*. New York: Mariner Books, 2004.

———. *The Blind Watchmaker: Why the Evidence of Evolution Reveals a Universe Without Design*. New York: Norton & Company, Inc., 1986.

Dean, J., and S. Ghemawat. "MapReduce: Simplified Data Processing on Large Clusters." *Communications of the ACM* 51, no. 1 (2008): 107–114,.

Della Sala, S. *Mind Myths. Exploring Popular Assumptions about the Mind and Brain* Chichester, UK: John Wiley and Sons, 1999.

Dennett, D. C. *Consciousness Explained.* New York: Little Brown & Co., 1981.

———. *Darwin's Dangerous Idea: Evolution and the Meanings of Life.* New York: Simon & Schuster, 1995.

Descartes, R. *The Philosophical Writings of Descartes.* Cottingham, J., Stoothoff, R., Kenny, A., and Murdoch, D., trans. Cambridge, MA: Cambridge University Press, 1988.

Donoghue, J. P. "Bridging the Brain to the World: A Perspective on Neural Interface Systems." *Neuron* 60, November 6 (3): 511–521, 2008.

———. "Limits of Reorganization in Cortical Circuits." *Cerebral Cortex* 7, no. 2 (1997): 97–99.

Donoghue, J. P., A. Nurmikko, M. Black, and L. R. Hochberg, "Assistive Technology and Robotic Control Using Motor Cortex Ensemble-Based Neural Interface Systems in Humans with Tetraplegia." *Journal of Physiology* 579, no.3 (2007):603–611.

Dowling, J. *The Great Brain Debate: Nature or Nurture?* Princeton: Princeton University Press, 2007.

Edelman, G. M. *Neural Darwinism: The Theory of Neuronal Group Selection.* New York: Basic Books, 1987.

Elsayed, T., J. Lin, and D. Oard. "Pairwise Document Similarity in Large Collections with MapReduce." *Annual Meeting of the Association for Computational Linguistics* 2, no. 46 (2008): 265–268.

Fellbaum, C. *WordNet: An Electronic Lexical Database.* Cambridge, MA: MIT Press, 1999.

Fiedler, K. "The Dependence of the Conjunction Fallacy on Subtle Linguistic Factors." *Psychological Research* 50 (1998): 123–129.

Fox, C. R. and Y. Rottenstreich. "Partition Priming in Judgment Under Uncertainty." *Psychological Science* 14 (2003): 195–200.

Gates, B. *Business @ the Speed of Thought.* New York: Warner Books, 1999.

Gigerenzer, Gerd. *Gut Feelings: The Intelligence of the Unconscious.* New York: Viking, 2007.

———. "The Irrationality Paradox." *Behavioral and Brain Sciences* 27 (2004): 336–338.

———. "How to Make Cognitive Illusions Disappear: Beyond Heuristics And Biases." *European Review of Social Psychology* 2 (1991): 83–115.

Gigerenzer, G., and U. Hoffrage, "How to Improve Bayesian Reasoning Without Instruction: Frequency Formats." *Psychological Review* 102 (1995): 684–704.

Gilovich, T., V. H. Medvec, and S. Chen, "Commission, Omission, and Dissonance Reduction: Coping with Regret in the Monty Hall Problem." *Personality and Social Psychology Bulletin* 21 (1995): 182–190.

Gladwell, M. *Blink: The Power of Thinking Without Thinking.* Boston: Back Bay Books, 2007.

———. *The Tipping Point: How Little Things Can Make a Big Difference.* Boston: Back Bay Books, 2002.

———. *Outliers: The Story of Success.* New York: Little, Brown and Company, 2008.

Goldberg, E. *The Wisdom Paradox: How Your Mind Can Grow Stronger as Your Brain Grows Older.* New York: Gotham Books, 2006.

Goldston, M. *The Turnaround Prescription: Repositioning Troubled Companies.* New York: Free Press, 1992.

Goleman, D. *Emotional Intelligence.* New York: Bantam Dell, 1997.

Gore, A. "Basic Principles for Building an Information Society." *Information, Communication & Education* 15, no. 2 (1996): 226–228.

Gould, S. J. *Full House: The Spread of Excellence from Plato to Darwin.* New York: Three Rivers Press, 1996.

Grove, A. *Only the Paranoid Survive.* New York: Currency Doubleday, 1996.

Haven, K. F. *Marvels of Science: 50 Fascinating 5-Minute Reads.* Englewood: Libraries Unlimited, 1994.

Hawkins, J. *On Intelligence.* New York: Times Books, 2004.

Hertwig, R., and G. Gigerenzer, "The 'Conjunction Fallacy' Revisited: How Intelligent Inferences Look Like Reasoning Errors." *Journal of Behavioral Decision Making* 12, no. 4 (1999): 275–305.

Higbee, K. L., and S. L. Clay, "College Students' Beliefs in the Ten-Percent Myth." *Journal of Psychology* 132, no. 5 (1998): 469–476.

Hinton, G. E., and J. A. Anderson, *Parallel Models for Associative Memory.* Hillsdale, NJ: Erlbaum Associates, 1981.

Hochberg, L. R., M.D. Serruya, G. M. Friehs, J. A. Mukand, M, Saleh, A.H. Caplan, A. Branner, D., Chen, R. D. Penn, and J. P. Donoghue, "Neuronal Ensemble Control of Prosthetic Devices by a Human with Tetraplegia." *Nature* 442, no. 7099 (2006): 164–171.

Hofstadter, D. *I Am a Strange Loop.* New York: Basic Books, 2007.

———. *Godel, Escher, Bach: An Eternal Golden Braid.* New York: Basic Books, 1999.

Hofstadter, D, and D. C. Dennett. *The Mind's I: Fantasies and Reflections on Self and Soul.* New York: Basic Books, 1981.

Hogan, J. *Mind Matters: Exploring the World of Artificial Intelligence.* New York: Del Ray Books, 1997.

Howells, W. *Getting Here: The Story of Human Evolution.* Washington, DC: Compass Press, 1992.

James, W. "The Energies of Men," *Science* 25, no. 635 (1907), 321–332.

———. *The Principles of Psychology.* New York: Henry Holt and Company, 1890.

Johnson, S. *Emergence.* New York: Scribner, 2001.

————. *Mind Wide Open*. New York: Scribner, 2004.

Johnson-Laird, P. N. *Mental Models: Towards a Cognitive Science of Language, Inference, and Consciousness*. Cambridge, MA: Harvard University Press, 1983.

Johnson-Laird, P. N., P. Legrenzi, V. Girotto, and M. S. Legrenzi, "Probability: A Mental Model of Extensional Reasoning." *Psychological Review* 106 (1999): 62–88.

Joseph, R. *The Naked Neuron: Evolution and the Languages of the Body and Brain*. New York: Plenum Press, 1993.

Kahneman, D., P. Slovic, and A. Tversky, eds.. *Judgment Under Uncertainty: Heuristics and Biases*. Cambridge/New York: Cambridge University Press, 1982.

Kahneman, D., and A. Tversky, "On the Psychology of Prediction." *Psychological Review* 80 (1973): 237–251.

Kandel, Eric R. *In Search of Memory: The Emergence of a New Science of Mind*. New York: W. W. W. Norton & Company, 2006.

Kaplan, R. S., D. P. Norton, S. D. Friedman, B. V. Krishnamurthy, T. J. Erickson, J. M. Stibel, and P. Delgrosso. "Unconventional Wisdom in a Downturn." *Harvard Business Review*, December 2008.

Keil, F. C., *Concepts, Kinds, and Cognitive Development*. Cambridge, MA: MIT Press, 1989.

Kidder, T. *The Soul of a New Machine*. New York: Atlantic-Little, Brown, 1981.

Kuhn, T. S. *The Structure of Scientific Revolutions*. Chicago: University of Chicago Press, 1962.

Kurzweil, R. *The Age of Spiritual Machines*. New York: Penguin Books, 2000.

————. *The Singularity Is Near*. New York: Penguin Books, 2005.

Lenat, D. B. "Cyc: Toward Programs with Common Sense." *Communications of the ACM* 33 (1990): 8.

Leroi-Gourhan, A. *Gesture and Speech*. Cambridge, MA: MIT Press, 1993.

Li, C., and J. Bernoff. *Groundswell: Winning in a World Transformed by Social Technologies*. Boston: Harvard Business Press, 2008.

Lichtenstein, S., and P. Slovic, "Reversal of Preferences Between Bids and Choices in Gambling Decisions." *Journal of Experimental Psychology* 89 (1971): 46–55.

Locke, J. *An Essay Concerning Human Understanding*. 1690. London: Guernsey Press Co. Ltd., 1977.

Malt, B. C. "Water is Not H_2O." *Cognitive Psychology* 27 (1994): 41–70.

Margolis, H. *Patterns, Thinking, and Cognition: A Theory of Judgment*. Chicago: University of Chicago Press, 1988.

McClelland, J. L., and D. E. Rumelhart, *Parallel Distributed Processing: Explorations in the Microstructure of Cognition*. Cambridge, MA: MIT Press, 1986.

Metcalfe, R. "Bob Metcalfe on What's Wrong with the Internet: It's the Economy, Stupid." *IEEE Internet Computing* 1, no. 2 (1997): 6–17.

Miller, G. A. "The Magical Number Seven, Plus or Minus Two: Some Limits on Our Capacity for Processing Information" *Psychological Review* 63, no. 2 (1956): 81–97.

———. "On Knowing a Word." *Annual Review of Psychology* 50 (1999): 81–97.

Minsky, M. *The Emotion Machine : Commonsense Thinking, Artificial Intelligence, and the Future of the Human Mind.* New York: Simon & Schuster, 2006.

Minsky, M. L., and S. A. Papert, *Perceptrons: An Introduction to Computational Geometry.* Cambridge, MA: MIT Press, 1988.

Montague, R. *Your Brain Is (Almost) Perfect: How We Make Decisions.* New York: Plume Books, 2007.

Moore, G. A. *Crossing the Chasm: Marketing and Selling Technology Products to Mainstream Customers.* New York: HarperBusiness, 1991.

Mountcastle, V. B. "Introduction: Computation in Cortical Columns." *Cerebral Cortex* 13, no. 1 (2003): 2–4.

Nozick, R. *Philosophical Explanations.* Cambridge, MA: Harvard University Press, 1981.

Ohanian, H. C. *Einstein's Mistakes: The Human Failings of Genius.* New York: W.W. Norton & Company, 2008.

O'Neill, E, B Lavoie, and R Bennett. "Trends in the Evolution of the Public Web 1998–2002," *D–Lib* 9 (2003): 4.

Philip, B. A., Y. Wu, J. P. Donoghue, J. N. Sanes. "Performance Differences in Visually and Internally Guided Continuous Manual Tracking Movements." *Experimental Brain Research,* 2008.

Pinker, S. *How the Mind Works.* New York: W.W. Norton & Company, 1997.

———. *The Blank Slate: The Modern Denial of Human Nature.* New York: Viking, 2002.

Pinker, S., and J. Mehler, eds.. *Connections and Symbols.* Cambridge, MA: MIT Press, 1988.

Plato. *The Collected Dialoguesof Plato, Including the Letters.* E. Hamilton and H. Cairns, eds. Trans. Lane Cooper and others. Princeton, NJ: Princeton University Press, 1961.

Plotnik, J. M., F. B. M. de Waal, and D. Reiss. "Self-Recognition in an Asian Elephant." *Proceedings of the National Academy of Sciences* 103 (2006): 17053–17057.

Posner, M. I., and M. E. Raichle. *Images of Mind.* New York: Scientific American Library, 1994.

Pottruck, D. S., and T. Pearce. *Clicks and Mortar: Passion-Driven Growth in an Internet-Driven World.* San Francisco: Jossey-Bass, 2000.

Putnam, H. *Representation and Reality.* Cambridge, MA: MIT Press, 1988.

Reis, A., and J. Trout. *Positioning: The Battle for Your Mind*. New York: McGraw-Hill, 1981.

Reiss, D., and L. Marino. "Mirror Self-Recognition in the Bottlenose Dolphin: A Case of Cognitive Convergence." *Proceedings of the National Academy of Sciences* 98 (2001): 5937–5942.

Rosch, E., and C. B. Mervis, "Family Resemblance: Studies in the Internal Structure of Categories." *Cognitive Psychology* 8 (1975): 382–439.

Russell, S. J., and P. Norvig. *Artificial Intelligence: A Modern Approach*. New York: Prentice Hall, Inc., 1995.

Ryle, G. *The Concept of Mind*. Chicago: University of Chicago Press, 2002.

Simon, H. A. "Information Processing Theory of Human Problem Solving." In W. K. Estes. ed., *Handbook of Learning and Cognitive Processes*, vol. 5. Hillsdale, NJ: Erlbaum, 1978.

Schiller, Robert. *Irrational Exuberance*. Princeton, NJ: Princeton University Press, 2000.

Schumpeter, J.A. T*he Theory of Economic Development: An Inquiry into Profits, Capital, Credit, Interest and the Business Cycle*. Cambridge: Cambridge University Press, 1934.

———. *Business Cycles*.

Serruya, M. D., N. G. Hatsopoulos, L. Paninski, M. R. Fellows, and J. Donoghue, "Instant Neural Control of a Movement Signal." *Nature* 416 (2002): 141–142.

Sloman, S. A., S. Over, and J. M. Stibel, "Frequency Illusions and Other Fallacies." *Organizational Behavior and Human Decision Processes* 91, no. 2 (2003): 296–309.

Smith, E. E., and D. L. Medin. *Categories and Concepts*. Cambridge, MA: Harvard University Press, 1981.

Sowell, T. *Knowledge and Decisions*. New York: Basic Books, 1980.

Stibel, J. M. "The Effects of Associativity, Interconnectivity and Generation on Memory." Thesis 39090010918650b. Medford, MA: Tufts University, 1995.

———. "The Role of Explanatory-based Feature Relations Among Artifact and Biological Kind Categorization." Graduate Dissertation 47191809. Providence, RI: Brown University, 1999.

———. "Getting the User to Ask the Right Question and Receive the Right Answer: A Cognitive and Linguistic Science Approach to Searching the Internet." *Proceedings of the Twenty-first National Online Meeting*, 21: 425–429, 2000.

———. "Mental Models and Online Consumer Behavior." *Behavior & Information Technology* 24, no. 2 (2005): 147–150.

———. "Increasing Productivity through Framing Effects for Interactive Consumer Choice." *Cognition, Technology & Work* 7, no. 1(2005): 63–68.

———. "The Role of Explanation in Categorization Decisions." *International Journal of Psychology* 41, no. 2 (2006): 132–144.

———. "Discounting Do's and Don'ts." *MIT Sloan Management Review* 49, no. (20071): 5.

———. "Categorization and Technology Innovation," in Harnad and Dror, eds., *Cognition Distributed: How Cognitive Technology Extends Our Minds*. Amsterdam: John Benjamins, 2008.

Stibel, J. M., I. E. Dror, and T. Ben-Zeev. "The Collapsing Choice Theory: Dissociating Choice and Judgment in Decision Making," *Theory and Decision* 66, no. 2 (2009): 149–179.

Surowiecki, J. *The Wisdom of Crowds: Why the Many Are Smarter Than the Few and How Collective Wisdom Shapes Business, Economies, Societies, and Nations*. New York: Doubleday, 2004.

Taleb, N. *The Black Swan: The Impact of the Highly Improbable*. New York: Random House, 2007.

Tancer, B. *Click: What Millions of People Are Doing Online and Why It Matters*. New York: Hyperion, 2008.

Tapscott, D., and A. Williams. *Wikinomics: How Mass Collaboration Changes Everything*. New York: Penguin, 2006.

Truccolo, W., G. M. Friehs, J. P. Donoghue, and L. R. Hochberg, "Primary Motor Cortex Tuning to Intended Movement Kinematics in Humans with Tetraplegia." *Journal of Neuroscience* 28, no. 5 (2008): 1163–1178.

Tversky, A. and D. Kahneman, "Extension Versus Intuitive Reasoning: The Conjunction Fallacy in Probability Judgment." *Psychological Review* 90, no. 4 (1983): 293–315.

———. "Judgment Under Uncertainty: Heuristics and Biases." *Science* 185 (1974): 1124–1131.

Vise, D. A., and M. Malseed. *The Google Story*. New York: Delacorte Press, 2005.

Williams, R. W., and K. Herrup. "The Control of Neuron Number." *Annual Review of Neuroscience* 11 (1988): 423–453.

Winograd, T., *Understanding Natural Language*. New York: Academic Press, 1972.

———. *Language as a Cognitive Process*. Reading, MA: Addison Wesley, 1983.

Winograd, T., and F. Flores. *Understanding Computers and Cognition: A New Foundation for Design*. Norwood, NJ: Ablex Publishing Corp., 1986.

Wisniewski, E. J. "Prior Knowledge and Functionally Relevant Features in Concept Learning." *Journal of Experimental Psychology: Learning, Memory, and Cognition* 21, no. 2 (1995): 449–468.

Wisniewski, E. J., and D. L. Medin, "On The Interaction of Theory and Data in Concept Learning." *Cognitive Science* 18 (1994): 221–281.

Zey, M. *The Future Factor: The Five Forces Transforming Our Lives and Shaping Human Destiny*. New York: McGraw-Hill, 2000.

I want to start by thanking anyone who took the time to read this book. Frankly, I wrote *Wired for Thought* primarily for myself—it was something I needed to do. I know it sounds selfish, but it's true. I do not make my living as an author. Writing this book was important to me because it helped synthesize my thoughts around a number of disparate fields that excite me: science, business, and technology. I often refer to myself as an *academic gone bad*: part scientist, part philosopher, but mostly an entrepreneur. I struggled to find a good balance between my passions and to convey what excites me about what I do every day. This book is the result and I hope you enjoyed it.

Acknowledgments are typically nothing more than an exhaustive list of obligatory "thank yous" and add little value to the actual book. Worse, there is no orchestra to speed an author along, such as the one you hear at the Oscars when an actor's speech invariably goes too long. In that vein, I will likely ramble on, so *feel free to stop reading here.*

It is clearly redundant to thank Dan Dennett and Jim Anderson (for that, simply read pages 1–231), but I have another mentor who received too little attention in this book. Dan Ariely was my adviser at MIT Sloan and is a long-time friend. It was Dan who introduced me to my literary agent and talked me into writing a book. He has done more for me and my career than I can ever hope to repay.

Whether by luck or coincidence, I had perhaps the best combination of publisher, editor, and agent that an author could ask for. Harvard Business School deserves special mention, not just because it is a preeminent publishing house, but also because it gave me the flexibility to write an atypical business book. This was in large part due to the efforts of Harvard's editorial director, Jacque Murphy. Without Jacque and the team at Harvard, this book could not have been completed. And without the help of my agent, Jim Levine, this project would have never made it off the ground. Jim and his superstar team did more to develop this book than any author should expect of his agent.

I had a long list of collaborators, but three stand out, as they participated in virtually every aspect of the book: Erik Calonius, Pete Delgrosso, and Cheryl Stibel. Erik is an award-winning editor who was once the bureau chief for *Newsweek*. He has spent time with some of the world's greatest minds and has edited countless articles and books, so I feel privileged to have Erik as a friend and colleague. In many ways, it is Erik's imprint on this book—from research to ideas to content—that makes it what it is; his contribution cannot be understated. Pete is a business executive who has worked with me at almost every company I have been a part of. He has as much insight into my businesses as does anyone, and he has contributed to each of their successes. He also had the misfortune of going to grade school with me, so other than my family, he knows me better than anyone. Pete did extensive research for the book, provided insight, case studies, and in many cases, ideas that added to the central thesis of the book. Finally, my wife Cheryl acted as my science adviser and helped create a personality and sense of balance for the book. Cheryl is a social psychologist by background and helped give the book its humanistic perspective. She is also my true inspiration (but more about that later).

The following people also gave up many hours of their time helping me with different aspects of the book, and making it better as a result: Dan Ariely, Massi Ciaramita, Roseann Duran, Reade Fahs, Mark Goldston, Judy Hackett, and David Landan. Many thanks as well to five peer reviewers whom Harvard selected. The review process is anonymous so I will collectively thank the reviewers whose comments—both kind and cruel—added to the quality, readability, and rigor of the book. I would also like to thank two reviewers independently, as each of them approached me after the process to provide additional feedback outside of the cloak of anonymity: Itiel Dror and Pamela Goldberg.

In addition to the people who spent time directly on the book, a number of people have influenced my thinking on business, science, and technology over the years: Paul Allopenna, Darlene Amar, Diana Anderson, Peter Arrowsmith, John Assaraf, Adam Bain, Jack Balousek, Brett Baris, Avi Ben-Zeev, Sheila Blumstein, Scott Bogdan, Bill Borzage, Doug Bross, David Brown, Vance Brown, Ron Burr, Mike Callahan, Bill Campbell, Colin Campbell, Mark Cannon, Jon Carder, Kevin Carney, Richard Cashio, Gene Charniak, Richard Chechile, Peter Christothoulou, Helen Clancey, Jeff Coats, Matt Coffin, Clint Coghill, Paul Conley, Sky Dayton, Kevin DeBré, Tobias Dengel, Dave Dickinson, John Donoghue, David Dowling, Andrew Duchon, Carl Dunham, Cliff Dutton, Reade Fahs, Finn Faldi, Jordan Fladell, Michael Fuchs, Dean Gels, Efrem Gerzberg, Heidi Gibson, Jon Goby, Phil Goldsmith, Mark Goldston, Brian Graham, David Greenberg, Jonathan Greenblatt, Joe Griffin, Danny Gumport, Gary Hall, Dan Handy, Nicho Hatsopoulos, Randy

Haykin, Randy Haykin, Barrett Hazeltine, Bill Heindel, Scott Hilleboe, Charles Hilliard, Mark Hodson, Rolla Hoff, Seymour Holtzman, Russ Horowitz, Gary Hromadko, David Hughes, Mike Janover, Mark Johnson, Paul Jordan, Mark Kaplan, Demetrios Karis, Tim Karman, Alex Kazerani, Ed Kelly, Tom Landauer, Bob Lee, Phil Lieberman, Mike Lunsford, Yvette Martinez, Michael Mathieu, Kenneth McBride, Matt McClure, John McIlvery, Nick McKay, George Miller, Jim Morgan, Chris Munro, Elliot Noss, Chris Nowlin, Larry Page, Sam Paisley, Barbara Palmer, Will Pemble, Jordan Pollack, Jerry Popek, Kamran Pourzanjani, David Rahmel, Fred Randall, Lock Reddic, Brent Reid, Steve Reiss, Ernie Riemer, Jim Riesenbach, Vikas Rijsinghani, Jim Risner, David Rosenblatt, Mark Ross, Ben Rubin, John Santini, Jeffrey Schwartz, Julie Sedivy, James Segil, Steve Sereboff, Bob Sezack, Eric Shashoua, Steve Siegal, Suren Singh, Peter Skopp, Steven Sloman, Sal Soraci, Jim Sorce, Aaron Stibel, Elaine Stibel, Gary Stibel, Joe Stubbs, John Suh, Joan Swanberg, Marc Tanner, Rusty Taragan, Mike Tarr, Jan Thomson, Jeff Tinsley, Gonzalo Troncoso, Doug Tutor, Bryan Whang, Joel Williamson, Jake Winebaum, Greg Wong, Brian Woods, Stanley Yang, and Dave Yanks.

For most people, it is the paycheck that drives them to work every morning. For me, it is the people. I have yet to find a great idea, an innovative technology, or a disruptive business model that can propel a company further faster than a great team. I have been lucky to work with some of the best in business, science, and technology, and want to thank each and every one of them. But at the risk of creating an endless list, I will acknowledge generally all of the executives, board members, and employees from Simpli, United Online (NetZero, Juno, Classmates.com), Worldwide MediaWorks, ThinMail, The Search Agency, Zeo, Axon Labs, Applied

Cognition Labs, MojoPages, Web.com, Interland, Website Pros, Autobytel, EdgeCast, and BrainGate. As it often turns out, many of the people at the above companies have worked with me more than once—and I extend a special thanks to those people whom I have had the pleasure of working with at two, three, even four companies together.

If it is the great people I work with that motivates me to come to the office each morning, it is my family that excites me to come home each night. My parents, brother, and relatives have always provided me with encouragement and passion. But my wife Cheryl is my true inspiration and a partner in everything I have done. She is kind, compassionate, and brilliant—the hardest part about writing this book was spending time away from her. She is also a wonderful mother to two of the best kids in the world. I can't think of anything more rewarding and fun than spending time with them.

INDEX

ABOUT THE AUTHOR

Jeffrey M. Stibel is a brain scientist and entrepreneur who has helped build numerous public and private companies. He is currently President of Web.com, a public company that helps entrepreneurs launch and grow their businesses on the Web. He is also Chairman of BrainGate, a brain implant company that allows people to use their thoughts to control electrical devices. He serves on the boards of a number of private and public companies, as well as academic boards for Brown and Tufts University. Stibel studied for his PhD at Brown University, where he was the recipient of the Brain and Behavior Fellowship, and studied business at MIT's Sloan School of Business.